GOOGLE BRAIN

Making Your Memoir a "Time Machine" on the Internet

Gordon Greb

iUniverse, Inc.
New York   Bloomington

GOOGLE BRAIN
Making Your Memoir a "Time Machine" on the Internet

Front and back cover illustrations by Jim Hummel

iUniverse books may be ordered through booksellers or by contacting:

iUniverse
1663 Liberty Drive
Bloomington, IN 47403
www.iuniverse.com
1-800-Authors (1-800-288-4677)

Because of the dynamic nature of the Internet, any Web addresses or links contained in this book may have changed since publication and may no longer be valid.

ISBN: 978-1-4401-8430-7 (sc)
ISBN: 978-1-4401-8428-4 (dj)
ISBN: 978-1-4401-8429-1 (ebk)

Printed in the United States of America

iUniverse rev. date: 12/8/2009

To my wife Darlene,
And to our own children,
And grandchildren,
Whose laughter has kept us young in heart and spirit.

Contents

Preface

The Meaning of Google

If I had only known, I would have been a locksmith.

—Albert Einstein (1879 – 1955)

I've recently discovered that each of us has a *Google Brain*. Mine has been telling me to dig into the past to give you everything you want to know. Having seen Silicon Valley come into being—living and working in San Jose, California, from the 1950s to the 1990s—I watched first-hand how computer technology advanced from a simple little game called "pong" on a home TV set to the mind-boggling services we take for granted today.

How it's changed our lives takes my breath away. I saw my first computer in the late 1970s and approached it tentatively, a bit apprehensive about how it worked. Then some small boys came along, marched right up to the computer keyboards, and began banging away. They didn't break it. No loud bells rang. Nothing horrible happened except a quiet humming. That's when I decided to buy one.

"Did you see that?" I said to my wife. "Those kids weren't afraid of it. We need one to keep up with the younger generation."

The fun of using my first computer, with its glowing screen and green typeface, was that it could be used like a typewriter, but besides writing letters, I also could play games and solve puzzles, provided I programmed everything myself. This required carefully typing a long string of instructions out of a book and saving this string onto a tiny floppy disc. Should I make the smallest mistake—that is, omitting a semi-colon, asterisk, or period from its proper place——I'd be stuck with a program that wouldn't run properly and I'd need to locate the error in order to make anything happen.

That was before IBM, Bill Gates, and Apple made things a lot easier. Still in the future were windows, the mouse, off-the-shelf software, and much, much more. Today millions of us "google" when we want to find something on the World Wide Web. That's when we use the widely popular automated search engine provided by Google, Inc., which does the task of finding what we want free of charge.

By copying every piece of information it can lay its hands on, Google has become the world's one-stop place for information. The company has proclaimed its intention to copy every single piece of information in the world, which possibly explains why its name comes from the term "googol," which the dictionary defines as the numeral one followed by one hundred zeros.

Comparing yesterday to today, we're now living in a computer wonderland. Our lives are changing rapidly as a consequence of these fabulous services. But that being said, I've now found something else that seems like a miracle, too—it's how my own mind operates and the way ideas pop into my head seemingly out of nowhere. In many ways my mental searches seem to resemble what is called "googling" on the Internet.

Before we had computers, we had to rely on our own brains to find what we were looking for. When I find myself using my grey matter to recall a particular incident, I'm astonished to discover that oftentimes the answer comes quickly to mind. Apparently the original thought is sent along the right pathways as electrical impulses to the proper places in my cranium and the order is carried out. However, the process also frequently fails and requires that I try other frustrating commands which may or may not work.

Even though the computer now triumphs over the brain in many ways, the contest is still not over. When Google finally has collected all the world's information in one place, the question still remains, "Who will it serve, the computer or human kind?" The computer revolution runs the risk of turning each of us into a Borg by collecting everything known about us for "Big Brother." As portrayed in the Star Trek television series, a Borg is a cybernetic organism, a computer-like machine that ingests a biological individual and keeps this human alive to serve its own needs.

Director Stanley Kubrick came up with a similar idea in his 1968 movie, *2001: A Space Odyssey*, when an astronaut is seen losing control of his spaceship because a computer named Hal, an artificial intelligence machine, decides to run things alone without human interference. Although a human being in this case succeeds in disabling Hal and regaining control, we may not be so lucky. Unless we're careful about the coming information-takeover, a Borg may get us if we don't watch out!

In the meantime I think we should concentrate on what human beings do with their own brains and the kind of responses we get from "googling." While we've been increasingly successful in augmenting our private and collective memories by artificial means, hopefully to keep us free, independent human beings and not slaves, we must be careful to insure that command and control rests with us and not with some outside person or agency.

Researchers in brain functioning show it is nearly impossible to recover exactly what you've experienced no matter how recent the event. A school of neuroscientists now believes that much of what you think you remember is recreated fiction. They've found that you never recall something exactly the same every time you try to do it. This is what French writer Marcel Proust found out even before scientists did. He left us one of the greatest efforts of self-analysis ever undertaken in his introspective study, *Remembrance of Things Past*. According to the conclusion of science writer Jonah Lehrer, what Proust noted about the human mind predated in many respects what modern neuroscientists are discovering today.

When I begin thinking about writing this book I ended up going through old trunks to recover things written in the past to supplement what lay in my cranial archives. However, as someone who witnessed the remarkable change in information gathering and dissemination in the twentieth century, I began to see the possibility of supplementing the printed word with the newer technology.

That's when I put my computer's search engine to work. Specifically, I started searching for sights and sounds of the past now available on the Internet, thanks to their having been saved on film, discs, tape, CDs, DVDs, and other modern devices. I spent endless days searching for anything online that would illuminate the story of my particular life, hoping to provide links in the bibliography when I found them. My plan was to make a "back to the future book"—an all-media recreation of the past—that would integrate my words-in-print with the vast archives of the Internet.

Although a more complete picture of the past is still in the future, I believe the day of fulfillment is rapidly approaching, as more data appears online. But as that moment arrives, there's the problem that many people wishing privacy won't want their personal lives and habits made public. Ideally each of us would like to control what the world sees and knows about us and choose for ourselves what we voluntarily want Google to digitize, such as what's been saved in diaries, books, films, photos, videos, tapes, CDs, DVDs, and other media devices. The uses to which we finally put the Internet will not be found easily. That's why I'm experimenting with one of them now.

For centuries the printed book was fixed and unchangeable, but in the digital age there is no reason why we can't change the way we use books. This will depend upon what's on the Web. Most printed books in the first decade of the twenty-first century are still scattered and confined to remote libraries—public and private—around the world. Ideally, all these books should be digitized, preserved on the Internet, and available to readers worldwide on our computers with proper copyright protection and compensation for their owners and creators.

If this book called *Google Brain* achieves anything, I hope it's that the print media can successfully merge with the Internet. In making my memoir an experimental "Time Machine" by using the resources online, I hope it proves interesting enough that it will encourage others to do try it. There can be wonderful surprises if you use the Google search engine to see what's there.

In my own case, for example, I was absolutely amazed to be able to see movies of Oakland, California, showing me moving images of people and places where I grew up in the 1920s and 30s. But what's now available is only a small fraction of what's needed for a fuller picture. If we are to get a more realistic appreciation of the past, the resources of the Internet must grow. As more becomes available, I believe it's one of the best ways of letting us understand "the way it was." But if we're going to go "back to the future," all of us must help to put it there.

With the Internet already offering us sights and sounds of the world never so easily available as now, the time has come to use this wonderful resource to better understand our own lives and future. We no longer need wait to apply what's there. As this vast reservoir of online data continues to expand and deepen, I believe it's possible right now to start creating an entirely new kind of book.

By showing that *Google Brain* can be linked to the Internet, I hope this experiment will inspire others to start "googling" and enjoy the pleasure of creating their own "Time Machine." If more of us try it, maybe we can show how an ordinary man's story can be enriched by a simple click of a mouse!

Linking the Book to the Internet

Because sights and sounds of the past can illuminate that particular time period, I recommend your using "Google Guide" at the end of each chapter. By using these links to the Internet, you'll be entering a simulated time machine, enabling you to better understand the book. Hopefully they also will let you see what Plato was talking about in his "Allegory of the Cave." The bulk of these links, however, will be found online at the book's web site, which, because the Internet is dynamic, may grow and change over time. The longer list is available in the reference section at http://www.googlebrainbook.blogspot.com/

GOOGLE GUIDE

Preface: The Meaning of Google

For related information, try these:

"The 'Google' Life" (CBS News).
http://www.cbsnews.com/video/watch/?id=4401791n&tag=content
Main;contentBody/

"Google's Master Plan" (film).
Find title at YouTube: http://www.youtube.com/

"History Detectives, Blue Print Special" (Gordon Greb on PBS).
http://www.pbs.org/opb/historydetectives/investigations/610_
blueprintspecial.html

For a longer listing, go to the book's web site:

Google Brain book: http://googlebrainbook.blogspot.com/

PART I

THE HUNGRY ID

*In the past,
nothing is irretrievably lost,
but rather, on the contrary,
everything is irrevocably stored
and treasured.*

——Viktor Frankl. *Man's Search for Meaning* (1984)

Chapter 1

The Dog Ate What?

If you want a friend in Washington, get a dog.

Harry Truman (1884-1972)

I'm expecting an invitation from the White House any day now. That's when President Barack Obama finally learns about something that vitally concerns him. But the problem is that he —like me—counts on the U.S. Post Office to deliver the mail through snow, rain, sleet, and hail. What worries me is simple: How will President Obama react when he finds out the postman doesn't always ring twice?

What I need to tell Obama is that two prized possessions have disappeared, one belonging to Mr. Obama himself and the other one to me. I call it—"The Case of the Missing Memoirs"—the president's and mine! If Winston Churchill were alive today he would describe it as "a riddle wrapped in mystery inside an enigma," worthy of an investigation by Agatha Christie, Sir Arthur Conan Doyle, or Raymond Chandler.

You may have bumped into this problem in the news but not paid much attention to it. You could have read about it in *USA Today*, seen it on C-SPAN, or heard it over National Public Radio. It's sort of a fever sweeping the country, affecting a huge number of people who have an absolute compulsion to be constantly scribbling, dictating, or clicking away. Each is trying to publish his or her memoir!

Among the 275, 232 writers who published new books last year, this group leads the pack—a long parade of greedy, media-generated fame-seekers, scrambling to be seen on television screens and the covers of *People* magazine. Look at this news item from the *Sacramento Bee*:

> JUNEAU (AP)—Alaska Gov. Sarah Palin is ready to tell her side, agreeing to publish a memoir with HarperCollins. The book will come out in spring 2010—the year she is up for reelection.

Joining her are other personalities in the news—the endless line of anxious actors, fading entertainers, successful crooks, and failed investors--all wanting to be interviewed by Terry Gross, Brian Lamb, or Charlie Rose. Each has been hoping to become the next Madonna, Jon Stewart, or Paris Hilton. Even pop stars recently locked up in prison are being pursued by publishers eager for exclusive rights to print their stories.

Memoir writing is such a widespread and common affliction these days that it could easily be classified as some kind of disease. Its symptoms are quite easy to notice. You need to look for individuals who are overwhelmed by the desire to tell you, or anyone who will listen, the complete story of their lives. Whenever you bump into someone like this—a person highly infected with Ego Mania—the advice given by medical specialists to friends, neighbors, and relatives is to simply treat each wild-eyed memory chaser as you would a little child. Say simply, "Why don't you go to your room and write it down?"

According to recent studies, it's not uncommon to see all of these highly motivated writers developing a high fever on Sunday mornings. They hop out of bed, run madly in search of the *New York Times*, and flip open the pages quickly to find the "Best Seller" book lists to see who's made it. What worsens their condition is news of celebrities making big bucks. A perfect example occurred in the case of Bill Clinton, notorious non-stop talker, who was paid $10.1 million one year for simply flying around the world telling people his life experiences, which earned him $3 million when published as a memoir. Even without newspaper publicity, they still keep popping up as guests on network television and radio shows. There's little escape from tub-thumpers of this kind.

Before discussing this further, I have a confession to make. It's that I, too, am a victim of this Memoir Revolution. I caught this malady early in life and it's left me with the most awful of symptoms. Day after day I have had a persistent need to come clean, spill the whole works, and tell the world what normal people would only tell their psychiatrists. Trying to understand why this has happened has become part of the memoir itself. It's kept me working harder and harder, hammering away at my keyboard and madly looking for the answer.

I first noticed this condition after Miss Crystal, my seventh grade teacher, read a book to us in class——*The Americanization of Edward Bok*——the true story about a Dutch immigrant boy, who arrives in America at age seven with his family from Holland knowing no English and succeeds in adapting to his new country. It was such a well-written autobiography that it left me with lasting memories of how Bok at sixteen became a close friend of Ulysses S. Grant, Henry Wadsworth Longfellow, and Oliver Wendell Holmes, and by the age of twenty-six, editor of one of the best-read women's magazines, the *Ladies Home Journal.*

At about the same time Edward Bok got me thinking about becoming a writer, I accidentally found another book, a weather-beaten copy of Henry Shute's *The Real Diary of a Real Boy* in an old trunk on my grandmother's farm. Inspired by Shute's primitive recollections of growing up in Exeter, New Hampshire, I began at the age of ten to try to write my own story the same way. I started writing my first diary during that summer's vacation, jotting down everything about chasing jackrabbits, climbing trees, and learning about bugs and things. It started a habit I've never been able to quit, and I've been hard at it ever since that time.

Something similar happened to Barack Obama before he moved into the White House. He sat down at a keyboard, collected his thoughts, and wrote his memoir, *Dreams from My Father.* They were recollections that gave a jump-start to his political ambitions, put him on the path to the U.S. Senate, helped persuade the Democratic Party to choose him as its nominee, and convince the American people to elect him as the country's forty-fourth President. As his supporter and fellow writer, I consider it a matter of high priority that I get to the White House to inform the President of my astounding news. Even though it will come as a shock, a dog owner has a "need to know." The President needs to know that a dog ate his memoir!

Certainly his own dog "Bo," a lively Portuguese water dog, wouldn't have done it. But the guilty culprit was one hungry enough to devour Obama's best seller——a new paperback edition of *Dreams from My*

Father—that I bought for $14.95 to send as a gift to my daughter. Since I had packaged it carefully, took it to the U.S. Post Office, and then found out she didn't get it, what do you suppose happened to it?

"Did you get the book?" I kept asking my daughter by phone.

"No, I didn't," she said repeatedly.

Then finally one day she called to say, "Yes, your package got here today but there's no book inside. It's torn open and empty."

If you think about it carefully, ask yourself which animals prefer to chase the postman every chance they get? The answer is obvious! Dogs, that's what. Obviously the mailman was chased, the dog grabbed the package, chewed it open, and buried the remnants of Obama's memoir in a deep hole somewhere. Until somebody at the U.S. Post Office can honestly explain what happened, a dog seems to be the most likely suspect in this important case.

As for my own missing memoir, the story is slightly different. Years ago I began working on my memoir only to have the entire narration scattered hither and yon in my writing room. My little Maltese puppy "Sugar" got into it and began chewing away at every piece of paper in sight. When the time came to try to put it back together again, I faced the insurmountable task of going through huge stacks of old letters, notebooks, photo albums, half-finished manuscripts, diaries, newspaper clippings, and documents of every kind.

Wondering how others dealt with problems like this, I stumbled across the business section of my local newspaper. There was a story telling how the U.S Treasury had been handing out billions of dollars to save banks, insurance companies, and troubled investment firms to keep them from bankruptcy. To get that money, all they had to do was ask. Why, I asked myself, don't writers get a fair share of this bounty? Writers like me need help in this depressed economy, too. It's time we were recognized as private entrepreneurs.

The truth is that writers are business people. Each of us is like the top CEO of any company, heavily involved in a "word manufacturing industry" and working hard at word management, idea development, and language investment strategy. We are private entrepreneurs who make the product ourselves, send it off to a factory to be mass-produced on an assembly line, and then retail it to the public like cans of beans, soft drinks, or chocolate-coated peanuts.

At tax time the Internal Revenue Service certainly considers writers small businessmen who work hard at planting the seeds of ideas, harvesting them from our fields of knowledge, and delivering them as bundles of words to a waiting market. We're as much a profit-making enterprise as any business run by a neighborhood Mom and Pop grocery store, a Fifth Avenue fashion designer, or Las Vegas casino operator. If the definition of a capitalist is someone who dares take a risk, then we writers are the bravest or most foolhardy of the bunch. Here is how our business of writing has been described by people engaged in it:

Dr. Samuel Johnson: "Any man who doesn't write for money is a fool."

Anthony Trollope: "As regards remuneration for the time to write a novel, stone breaking would have done better."

Thomas Hardy: "A man who writes stands up to be shot at."

Clarence Darrow: "Some day I hope to write a book, where the royalties will pay for the copies I give away."

Henry David Thoreau: "I have now a library of nearly nine hundred volumes, over seven hundred of which I wrote myself."

John Steinbeck: "The profession of book writing makes horse racing seem like a solid, stable business."

As anyone can see, I am struggling to complete my memoir and I am as needy as any firm on Wall Street being handed a big check by Uncle Sam to keep on going. To rescue me from my unfortunate case of "blankruptcy"—a sudden loss of memory, which denies me the chance to complete my book—I need a nice fat loan of a million dollars from Uncle Sam. Such a sum would tide me over the bumps, vastly improve my credit rating, and give me the confidence to go back to my computer keyboard to finish the business of completing my *Great American Memoir.*

If you are still reading this, please write your Congressmen to help. Tell your representative that the treasury department needs to help us writers. Otherwise those struggling with long sentences may get it into their heads to start another *Mutiny on the Bounty,* believing, of course, that the pen is mightier than the sword.

Post Script

What if my letter to Barack Obama fails to reach the White House? If that should happen, I'll e-mail the president's chief of staff, requesting an appointment to see Mr. Obama. It will be the only way to assure him he that needn't worry, because CEO Eric Schmidt of Google, Inc. already has his organization in Silicon Valley busily engaged in completing the great Google Book project. Soon they'll have all of our books—which will include *Dreams from My Father*—locked safely away in the world's largest online library, completely assuring security for all books for all time to come.

"Don't worry, Mr. President," I'll tell the chief executive when we meet. "Your book is perfectly safe. Incidentally, may we talk for a few minutes about why some of us needy writers could use some of your bailout money—?"

GOOGLE GUIDE

Chapter 1: The Dog Ate What?

For related information, try these:

"Meet the Obama Dog" 03/30/2009 (White House parody).
http://whitehouse.gov1.info/blog/blog_post/blog-obama-dog.html

"Tales of Yore: The Mail Carrier's Revenge," by Mark J. Woodbury. (book). Find title at Barnes and Noble: http://search.barnesandnoble.com/booksearch/

"Dreams from My Father: A Story of Race and Inheritance," by Barack Obama. (book). Find title at Google Books: http://books.google.com/

For a longer listing, go to the book's web site:

Google Brain Book: http://googlebrainbook.blogspot.com/

Chapter 2

Mind the Gap

With sixty staring me in the face, I have developed inflammation of the sentence structure and a definite hardening of the paragraphs.

——James Thurber (1894-1961)

The following is what I found when rummaging around in that old trunk looking for records of my travel and meal expenses while preparing my tax returns. I spotted a worn and tattered notebook amidst the clutter of my office. When I opened it, there lay a diary that could have been written by Socrates 2,400 years ago, that Greek philosopher who often advised his students to "know thyself."

I finally recognized the writing as my own. I had written it and then forgotten all about it. It seemed quite apropos since I've lately been depressed trying to remember the Stock Market Crash of l929, the Great Depression, World War II, Rock 'n' Roll, the Beatles, Vietnam, and Bush's Folly. I reasoned maybe this diary should be treasured as some kind of insight into a mind gradually fading away. It is in that spirit that I've chosen to admit these failings in this book.

==========o0o=========

Tuesday, February 6

Lately I've learned something shockingly new about myself. I'm beginning to forget small things. It is frustrating because these are mental losses of trivia which used to come easily to mind. My memory was good all of my life and my secret ambition had been to write an autobiography someday—remembering enough to set down a volume of interesting stories I took for granted. But now I realize it's something that can't be postponed.

Noting that today is Ronald Reagan's birthday, I am forced to consider a worse case scenario, which would be Alzheimer's disease, a terrible affliction that eventually robs a person of all he once knew and returns the mind to babyhood. I hope my condition is something less. I pray it's nothing serious, as what comes up missing in memory right now so far hasn't been anything too important, just names of people and places which are not part of my regular life anyway.

Do we really need to remember the names of long-gone movie stars of the 1930s and 40s, or street names of my old hometown, which have nothing to do with the way we live today? Once upon a time, facts and dates and names of people came trippingly to my tongue and without any furrowing of brow. Now it's somewhat surprising that I have to struggle, use word association, or other tricks, to bring these things to mind. I have to keep in mind that Albert Einstein once said, "Knowing where to find what you need in a book is more important than trying to remember everything."

Wednesday, February 7

Today I can safely say, "I've got six months to go." To what? Well, my next birthday, for one thing. While it may seemingly be an ordinary day of the year, it actually marks the exact mid-point between my birthdays—the time six months ago when I reached age 79 and the day coming up this year when I will attain the age of 80. There's no guarantee I'll get there, but the odds seem to say it's close enough to begin planning. I might as well look forward to its happening and then see exactly what happens.

The other day I met a lady on a bus who will be 81 this year. She said, "It's funny but I don't feel different from when I was young. I feel the same inside." She had to use a cane, walked with great difficulty, and needed help getting on and off the bus. Obviously her physical condition had not changed her self-image. Will my thoughts be the same? Do advancing years ever change how you feel about yourself? Will attaining 80 be significant? Knowing that there are people now in their 90s living a happy life keeps me going and looking forward to the same kind of future.

When I was very young, 40 seemed without question to be an advanced age. But on reaching it, I like most people, easily regarded it as the start of middle age. Because we keep busy, the years go by and then suddenly, there you are, having to face up to the fact you're nearly 60. However, this age may seem to be "good news" if you're healthy. New possibilities can be found in retirement, which, for an American with a good pension plan, means the freedom to do whatever you've always wanted to do in your spare time.

In many ways you can welcome becoming 60 or 65 because you'll be able to indulge yourself in a grand variety of leisure time activities, and join others your age who are doing the same. For many old people, this period of life means the first real freedom they've ever had. The term Old Age Pensioner (which has been used by the British to describe their old folks) hardly applies in the United States if you're happy and healthy approaching 70 and the thought of 80 seems far, far away.

Well, if the years go by and if Old Father Time is kind, you laugh at the pages being torn from your book of life. If you have been really blessed, you've inherited good genes, found a good family doctor, had regular medical checkups, followed a proper diet, and exercised regularly. If you've been lucky enough to miss out on fatal accidents, the possibility of reaching 80 seems to be a real possibility. With luck and pluck (as Horatio Alger, Jr., famous boys' book author, would put it) it's another age I hope to reach. Recording my thoughts along the way and reflecting on what went before are the objectives of this diary.

Sunday, February 18

Thoughts: I've now decided to put them down willy nilly as they come. Attempting to write perfect prose often stops me from writing as I try to make every sentence perfect. I lose the flow. So I'll just let the thinking roll and come back for proper editing later. Right now I'm thinking of creating my own Web site (courtesy of Google, Inc.) on the

Internet. Have found some very good personal sites. Realize the great big world out there is filled with people of all kinds. Some are greatly talented. Many are not. One needs to pick and choose to find what's truly worthwhile on the Internet.

I realize, after looking at a number of personal web pages—some for family associations, teen-agers, or folks starting small businesses—a vast number of people are doing it. But why do we do it? The word "ego" comes to mind. Is that why we do it? I've been thinking lately of doing a memoir in three parts: My life as (1) Ego, (2) Super Ego, and (3) Id.

While borrowing from Sigmund Freud, I will give each of these categories my own interpretation:

Ego, for example, is my ordinary self and the one I hope is presented to the outside world for approval, self-esteem, and various human rewards. Most autobiographies are in this category, where the inner self is carefully guarded and wants to put his/her best foot forward, not telling everything frankly and openly. Generally speaking, whenever you publish your life story, reveal it in an interview, or even put it on a Web site, you hope the feedback is positive, not negative.

Example: I wanted to be a cartoonist as a boy because they made big money doing something which was enjoyable and fun. When a nationally syndicated newspaper published my prize-winning drawing one Sunday and I got fan mail from young people (mostly girls) from several parts of the country, it was a terrific boost to my ego. How terrific to be famous! And I was still a young teenager.

Super Ego, to continue, would be the conscience you've developed in a lifetime. Some have more of it than others, but it is the inner voice judging and cautioning your current thoughts and behavior, as well as those of the past. Writers who give readers a bit of this thinking often attract readers because it's exciting to cross the barriers into the mind of others.

James Harvey Robinson summed up his life as a historian showing how people generally acquire attitudes, opinions, and judgments, which they cling to tenaciously, despite the fact many of them were acquired accidentally. See his book, *The Mind in the Making* (1921) for how this happens.

My Super Ego probably is the result of Super Parenting, where Mom and Pop told me what was right and what was wrong. They created the Jiminy Cricket voice, aided by my religious upbringing (Roman Catholic), formal public school education, friends, relatives, and associates, and lifelong reading. Society also plays a big role in dealing with how we think and behave, as schools, churches, politicians, and commercial interests go after our beliefs, votes, and money.

The Id is what we know the least about. Most autobiographies skip its influence entirely, unless seeking to attract readers by sensational revelations. Here is where one finds what the Greek philosophers call the appetites—hunger for food, sex, pleasure, entertainment, and power. These strong desires can cause a lot of turmoil and anxiety as the Super Ego argues, "No," and the Id says, "Yes." They're often the hardest to reveal. We seldom confess having them. Sometimes we don't even know we have them.

Because this story has three parts—a beginning (Id), middle (Ego), and ending (Super Ego)—please give me a minute to put my *Google Brain* in gear, wake up a few lazy neurons, and find out how this whole thing got started.

GOOGLE GUIDE

Chapter 2: Mind the Gap

For related information, try these:

"On the Sunny Side of the Street" -Ted Lewis – 1930 (song). Find title at YouTube: http://www.youtube.com/

"'See America First,' Oakland, California – 1931" (film). http://www.archive.org/details/SeeAmeri1931/

"The U.S. Grant Connection: Sept. 1, 2008," by Gordon Greb (column). http://www.thecolumnists.com/greb/greb51.html/

For a longer listing, go to the book's web site:

Google Brain Book: http://googlebrainbook.blogspot.com/

Chapter 3

Start Googling Now

Is Groucho your real name?
No, I'm breaking it in for a friend.

Groucho Marx (1895-1977)

The morning I landed on planet earth, everybody thought I was a little mouse and unfortunately frightened a lot of people at the wedding. Furthermore, it led people in authority in the big city of Oakland into believing I was an alien from outer space or perhaps an "undocumented person." Although all of these impressions were wrong, they began the very day I arrived in the small town of Irvington, California.

As you can see, the stork had made a mistake. Blame it on excitement, confusion, or carelessness, but my birth that Sunday morning at this old farmhouse not only surprised everybody but also came back years later to haunt me in a strange and devious way. How was I to know there would be future consequences when the Federal Express Big Bird miscalculated by dropping me off at the "Old Home Place" at this unanticipated address? My arrival that morning not only surprised people but also started a very unlikely chain of events.

First of all, it put a complete stop to the wedding. Before the minister could open his Bible, someone rushed into the room with the news, shouting, "Shouldn't we call a doctor?" Well, that was easier said than done. There was no telephone, the doctor's office was two or three miles away, and someone would need to get him. Fortunately, one of the male wedding guests volunteered to play Paul "The Baby is

Coming" Revere and galloped into town, knocked on the front door, and announced, "Irene's baby is coming!" Needing no further urging, Doctor Ormsby got his bag, hitched up his one-horse shay and hurried to the bedside as fast as his steed could carry him.

As far as the wedding ceremony was concerned, it had to be postponed till my coming-out party was over. Oh, I hope you weren't thinking the wedding was that of my mother. No, sir. Perish that thought! These nuptials were to be those of another young woman who was marrying my mother's brother. My mom had come as a bridesmaid. Anyway, my loud and dramatic entrance stole the spotlight away from the lovely bride-to-be. In no time at all, I had nearly the entire wedding party gathered around me, saying, "Oh, what a beautiful baby!" or "Isn't he adorable?" This is what's known as upstaging. And with that flair for drama, one wonders why this baby wasn't destined to appear on the silver screen as an actor like Cary Grant, George Clooney, or Liam Neeson.

Yes, I assumed that my rightful place was in the White House, since I started out exactly the same way as Abraham Lincoln. Both of us had been born in log cabins. That's because it was my grandfather had sawed the wood and cut the timbers to build the house of my birth and aroused my hopes. But the Cruel Witch of the East was stirring her pot that day and heckling, "You're not going to be eligible for the White House, dearee! Your destiny will be something else. I'll see to that".

Years passed. I'd been known for a lifetime by my teachers in school as "that funny little Greb kid." And that's who I remained until the 1940s, when I was forced to come face to face with the truth about me. It was just as Shakespeare had said long ago, "All the world's a stage and all the men and women merely players." I had lived a lifetime pretending to be somebody named *Whatzizname,* when in fact, like the great bard himself, I really could have been—well, let's say, Cary Grant, Ronald Reagan, or Brad Pitt.

Some people have said Shakespeare was really the Earl of Oxford or possibly the talented Mr. Christopher Marlowe. Therefore I, too, could turn out to be someone other than who I was supposed to be. When the truth finally came out—it was uncovered not by the FBI or the Better Business Bureau—but by my own efforts to join the military service after Pearl Harbor. Believe it or not, when I hoofed it down to the Alameda Courthouse to obtain a copy of my birth certificate, the clerk could not find it. He looked and looked and could not find a single birth record with my name. This came as a terrible shock.

By lacking a birth certificate, I could not claim to be a citizen, wave the flag, and demand that the government cut my taxes. Despite the fact my parents had always told me I had been delivered to this world in an old farmhouse in Irvington, the clerk couldn't find proof that what I was saying was true.

"What was that name again?" he and other office workers kept asking. Since I had not yet learned from army experience the colorful language to use to vent my frustration, I was determined to remain calm. But when I finally did blurt out some honest words of pure astonishment, these expletives did not, in fact, seem to shock the ears of anyone present. Maybe all these clerks had served in the military, a police department, or on a football team? No matter.

I could not properly comprehend what they were telling me at the courthouse anyway. Now that my true identity was being questioned I was beginning to ask myself, "Who am I?" and "Where did I come from?" Uppermost in my mind was the thought, "Why didn't my parents tell me I was adopted? Why had they shielded me from the truth all those years?" Now that I'd accidentally stumbled on the truth, what was I to do? If I am an orphan, what is my real name?

Fortunately, the clerical staff did not quit looking but continued combing through its files. Perhaps they took pity on this tall, skinny kid, who was barely dry behind the ears because he appeared to be clean-cut and honest individual. So they didn't dismiss me out of hand. Instead they tried to calm my fears while quietly opening drawers, searching through logs, and puzzling over what they were finding. While I rested my elbows on the counter in a mild state of shock, I began wondering whether to call myself Little Orphan Annie, Anthony Adverse, or Alexander Hamilton, whose true ancestries were somewhat in doubt.

Then I heard a soft voice say, "Come here. Look at this, Henry."

It seemed someone finally had made a fortunate discovery after one of the clerks blew dust off a birth certificate with the name baby "Goal" and found that the information matched exactly what I had been telling them. It recorded an infant being born in the little town of Irvington, California, the very day I arrived. After all, Irvington was a tiny town with a population of approximately five hundred people, and it wasn't accustomed to having babies arriving every day.

As the office workers studied this particular birth certificate, the document itself began to reveal how my problem had begun. It had turned up missing because someone earlier had been unable to comprehend the doctor's quickly scribbled, hard-to-read penmanship. After Doctor Ormsby had signed the form and sent it off, the receiving clerk entered the name in a logbook and then routinely filed it away. Obviously the clerk made his best guess concerning the baby's name. And it was wrong.

Twenty years later the world found me—together with the clerks in the office—studying the doctor's handwriting. Done in haste, the scrawls on that piece of paper could be read only with great difficulty. One person thought the name was "groan," another said it looked like "gulp," and a third insisted it resembled "grape." Perhaps that's what had frustrated the recording clerk long, long ago. And after weighing the possibilities, this anonymous clerk finally had identified me as baby "Goal." So into the records it went.

Was my problem over? Unfortunately not. The hard and cruel jaws of the law had sunk their teeth into me and wouldn't let go. The county clerk could not merely tear up the incorrect documents and create new. For years I had been listed in the records incorrectly as Goal. And now that we had found this official mistake, somebody needed to do something about it.

So my folks hired an Oakland lawyer. He had my parents sign a sworn statement that assured the State of California that I was legitimately the child of Mr. and Mrs. Greb, whose baby had been born at the place and date stated. This officially became my name day. Henceforth nobody could doubt that I was the person the stork had brought by special delivery and had a constitutional right to run for the presidency. After everything was notarized, signed, sealed, and delivered, the powers-that-be finally untangled that twisted web of woe and allowed me to be legally sworn into the service of Uncle Sam in World War II.

"Whew! I'm in the army now," I thought. "At last I am safe."

It was comforting to know that my dog tags now had my correct name. Thus if my luck ran out and I happened to run into a bullet on the battlefield I wouldn't be an unknown soldier to be shipped home to be interred in Grant's Tomb or some place like that. How lucky can you get?

GOOGLE GUIDE

Chapter 3: Start Googling Now

For more on this subject, try these:

"King of Jazz: Part 1 of 3" Bing Crosby with Rhythm Boys. (song). Time: 2:07 min. Find title at YouTube: http://www.youtube.com/

"Oakland, California -1928" (film). http://www.archive.org/details/OaklandC1928/

"Will Rogers on the Radio – Unemployment" (recording). Time: 2:45 min. Find title at YouTube: http://www.youtube.com/

For a longer listing, go to the bookís web site:

Google Brain Book: http://googlebrainbook.blogspot.com/

Chapter 4

It's a Jungle Out There

Although this work is history, I believe it to be true.

—Mark Twain (1835-1910)

As a child, world events didn't interest me in 1929. Certainly few children paid much attention to what was going on. Only later did we learn about the great Wall Street crash on October 24, 1929, which became known thereafter as "Black Thursday." Although it caused a deep economic depression, none of us kids knew its importance at the time. Few adults knew also. Those that did, didn't know which way to turn. Everyone seemed baffled on how to solve what turned into a deepening and devastating problem.

In Germany, Adolf Hitler was using the crisis to his own advantage, moving step by step with his Nazi party to seize control in Germany and expanding his country's military-industrial power as a means of returning prosperity to his homeland. Soon our own country was destined to come under the leadership of Franklin Delano Roosevelt, who despite being paralyzed by polio, would use democratic government to rescue the poor and unemployed. He first saw the need for a state relief agency as new governor of New York and later as chief executive of the nation.

As children, we knew nothing of this. We only paid attention to what was happening around our own homes, neighborhoods, or schools. There was little time for newspaper articles or headlines. We had our own games to play and the adults had theirs. When the afternoon newspaper was thrown on my front porch, I ran to get "the funnies," tossing the news sections aside for the latest adventures of *Buck Rogers, Dick Tracy,* and *Little Orphan Annie.*

When we moved to East Oakland in 1923, it was a newly developed area of the city, a pleasant neighborhood near shopping, schools, and transportation. Our wood-framed residence at 2615 64th Avenue was a newly built, cream-colored, one-story house, with two-bedrooms and one bath. We had acacia and plum-cot trees planted out front. Our family doctor who made house calls said he always enjoyed coming to 64th Avenue because of all the trees. They were concentrated near the east end of the block, between Foothill Boulevard and East 14th Street, where we lived. Every house was attractive in its own way because contractors in those days put up one building at a time, large subdivisions had not yet been thought of.

I was two years old and have no memory of leaving our first home on Adams Street, near Lake Merritt, close to where my father had established his business on Broadway. That small house has since been torn down and an apartment stands in its place. Pop decided to move his tire shop to the Melrose district of East Bay to put it closer to customers driving along busy East 14th Street.

During this time our teachers at Whittier Elementary School watched over us carefully. They must have wondered what would become of us. Often they shook their heads to let us know of their displeasure over our seeming indifference to education. Yet they somehow kept our restless young bodies firmly fixed to our seats in school and devised innovative ways to cram enough skills and information into our heads to get us promoted to the next grade. We were constantly told, "Children, you must work hard to get good grades because it's important for your future." Good advice. But we rarely took it.

What actually influenced us was what we observed in our parents and teachers. This subliminal recognition of their behavior was actually what counted the most. I now realize it was the way these adults behaved every day that somehow was picked up by our subconscious minds and slowly seeped into our own characters. We saw that they were honest, decent, and caring people.

When the United States declared war on Germany in 1917, my twenty-one year old father was healthy, single, and because of his

German-American ancestry, determined to prove his patriotism. Although well employed as a clerk for the Southern Pacific Company on Market Street in San Francisco, he volunteered for the U.S. Army almost immediately. He took his basic training at Camp Lewis, Washington, was assigned to the 18th Engineers railway regiment and shipped overseas, finding himself among the first of the Yankees to arrive in France. Soldiers in his unit included newspapermen Wood Soanes, of the *Oakland Tribune,* and Harold Ross, of the *San Francisco Examiner,* who later founded *The New Yorker* magazine. The regiment's responsibility was to keep supply trains running to the front lines throughout the war.

After serving briefly with the railway outfit and then briefly trying the officer training program, newspaperman Ross went AWOL to find something better, joined the staff of *Stars and Stripes* in Paris, and finished his service writing about the war from behind the lines. My father, who was stationed near the front, saw Paris on a twenty-four hour pass at the end of the war. His letter home, describing Paris on a one-day leave, appeared in a weekly newspaper published in Oakdale, California, and was the highlight of his journalistic career. My dad had been recommended for promotion from sergeant to second lieutenant in the autumn of 1918 but the Armistice was signed before he could pin the commissioned officer's bars on his uniform.

Honorably discharged and back home, Brevet (the term means brief) Lt. W.H. Greb wasted little time in wooing petite Irene Agnes Benbow away from her family farm in Irvington. They soon agreed on a wedding date but before tying the knot, the new couple had to solve a problem. When war veteran Greb came back to reclaim his old job at the Southern Pacific Company in San Francisco, the firm had no job for him. Employers had no legal obligation in those days to rehire war veterans who were former employees.

So young Walter had to find another way to make a living. Earlier in life he and his father had run a fleet of jitney buses from San Francisco to San Jose. Now that the war was over, he believed the automobile business had a promising future. Seeing that the wheels of motorcars ran on rubber, he decided to open a tire shop in downtown Oakland (which, with luck, could have become a successful lifetime business).

His hunch was right because Walt's Tire Shop was profitable right up to the 1929 crash.

Pop was a self-made man. He was forced to drop out of high school by his own father who wanted him to help on their farm in Newark, California. But believing this was unfair, young Walter rebelled and ran away from home at the age of fourteen. What prompted him to do this was that he had loved school, winning praise from the county superintendent of schools, who announced after visiting Washington Union High School and conducting an oral examination of the class, "Walter Greb is the best historian in Alameda County."

A man who loved to read, especially American history, the life of Abraham Lincoln, and the U.S. Constitution, he never finished formal schooling but was self-educated. Whenever he found the opportunity, Pop could be seen with his nose in a book, magazine, or newspaper, always reading. Having had an early ambition to go into business, he saved enough money to buy a course in bookkeeping and commerce from a mail order house and then taught himself touch typing by studying the manual.

At the time his father forced him to leave school, young Walter Greb was a good pupil, fine writer, keen mathematician, and avid reader, who rode a mule eight miles round-trip each day in order to attend classes. But when his father insisted he become a farm hand and drop out of high school, it led to an argument in which they came to blows and the young teen-ager packed up his clothes and set out on his own, which ended his academic career. By the time Grandfather Greb and Pop were reconciled, my dad had gone through the University of Hard Knocks, where he found out weaklings have little chance, brains are superior to brawn, and you should never let anyone push you around.

Soon after his tire shop business failed, my father applied for work at Southern Pacific Company as a locomotive fireman. But the company had no new jobs in 1930. The Depression had hit the railroad industry first, then agriculture, and finally businesses of every kind. Occasionally the railway needed him, but days of being called to work were rare and the duration of his employment temporary. Pop's main hope was that someday it would be permanent.

From the day he became a railway man, Pop had never touched intoxicating liquor. He said, "When I'm in the cab of a locomotive, responsible for the lives of the passengers we're carrying, I never want the smell of liquor on my breath in case of an accident." Alcohol never touched my mother's lips either. Nobody she knew of her Irish-English ancestry ever drank alcohol and she never so much as put a drop of wine in her cooking to flavor it. Mom was a complete teetotaler.

Railroading was my dad's first love. This was surprising because baby Walter's first sight of a train gave him a terrible fright. As a small boy holding the hand of his mother, he was frightened when he first saw a giant snorting monster chugging down the tracks into the station at St. Louis, Missouri. He never forgot that experience, the sight of such a dark menace coming with such smoke, noise, and huge spinning wheels. Perhaps a Freudian interpretation of his psyche would be that he needed to conquer that monster to prove he was a brave man.

Perhaps the same can be said for all small children. Why does Halloween appeal so much to them? Symbolized by ghosts and goblins, this particular holiday seems to have been designed especially for the young. It's the one night of the year when kids become strong in their imaginations as soldiers, kings, monsters, princesses, movie stars, goblins, or ugly creatures from the underworld. Wearing frightful masks and colorful costumes, children acquire special powers. On Halloween night they can go "trick or treating" down the street, looking for opportunities to scare people and being rewarded with candy by simply threatening to use their powers.

None of us knew, however, that 1929 was to be our last make-believe Halloween. It would be a long time before "Happy Halloween" had any real meaning for my generation. Unbeknownst to us, the whole world was becoming a spook house in real life and life-threatening forces were about to challenge the very existence of our families, our nation, and millions of people on earth. Due to stupid miscalculations by those in charge of big governments, along with bankers, investors, industrialists, economists, editorial writers, military leaders, and theorists, humankind was taken in the wrong direction. We were thrust into a worldwide catastrophe.

If my generation learned any lessons from those days, I think it's that we must be very careful in pandering to charismatic leaders and causes. The wrong leader can mean disaster. When America's Wall Street collapsed in 1929 it was bad enough at home, but it also was felt in Europe and Asia. Germany was particularly hard hit as industries faced closure, exports fell, and unemployment rose.

For Adolf Hitler, this was exactly what he wanted. His Nazi party had lost momentum, was unable to attract a majority of voters and seemed destined to remain in the dustbin of history. The market collapse of 1929 gave him a chance to whip up renewed enthusiasm for his fascist movement, to recover from a failed Munich coup d'etat attempt in 1924, which had jailed him for nine long months.

However, with this sudden economic disaster sending the country into turmoil, it put Hitler into a position to blame Germany's Weimar Republic and offer the Nazi party as the fatherland's only logical alternative. Huge audiences roared with enthusiasm as he toured the cities. Their desperate needs gave Hitler exactly what he wanted—the power of a dictator. With single-minded purpose he transformed Germany into a Frankenstein monster, a regimented society with a military regime, which set out to conquer the world.

As our American economy worsened, President Herbert Hoover's administration had no practical solutions. Apparently Hoover felt that by waiting long enough it would go away. But too many destitute Americans were facing starvation and could not wait. Unrest was building to a fever pitch. In the spring of 1932, Congress got a secret message from Hoover urging that the salaries of U.S. soldiers, sailors and marines not be cut, saying troops might be needed to put down a revolution.

That summer, fifteen thousand unemployed First World War veterans, desperately in need of help, gathered in Washington, D.C. and encamped on the capital's vast open mall. They had come from all over the USA to petition the government for bonuses authorized and promised by Congress for their honorable service, but the money was not to be paid them until 1945, thirteen years off. Among them was the father of my best friend Jack Corbett of Oakland, who had served in the trenches in France during the war and now had nowhere to turn for help except to his own government.

Desperately needing money to live on, these veterans begged for it now. But Hoover closed the White House, refused to see them, and ordered his chief of staff, General Douglas MacArthur, to mobilize the Army to forcibly remove them. Skirmishes broke out between hundreds of these seasoned vets and the regulars but the old soldiers did not revolt. They went home. They were merely patriotic Americans wanting help, not to incite a revolution.

With the nation in crisis, Democrats needed someone who could win the presidency and restore prosperity to America. When the delegates chose Franklin Delano Roosevelt, he electrified the convention by breaking precedent and flying to Chicago to personally address the delegates and accept his nomination. Standing before these wildly enthusiastic supporters, Roosevelt told them and a national radio audience: "I pledge to you, I pledge myself, to a new deal for the American people."

Then the band struck up what was to be the theme song of his campaign, *Happy Days Are Here Again*. In November, the results were in. Roosevelt had been elected the country's 32nd U.S. President, swept into office with 472 electoral votes to Hoover's 59, carrying all but six of the 48 states.

These are the details I had to learn later. In 1929 my concern was what to do on Halloween to celebrate with my family, schoolmates, and neighbors. Looking back I can still remember two small boys coming up the street that night, carrying jack-o-lanterns to light their way. They were my school chums in costume—nine-year old Jack Corbett and his cousin Arthur Corwin—who had come to enjoy my party. Counting my four-year old brother Wallace and myself, we were a little party of a not more than a half dozen kids enjoying ice cream and cake served by my mother.

Although we didn't know it, a hazardous future awaited us. Sooner than anyone could imagine we would need to stand strong against two unimaginable threats to our very own survival—a people-eating hobgoblin known as the Great Depression and after that, a fire-breathing monster wanting to devour us in World War II. As things turned out, Roosevelt became our most welcome "treat" and Hitler, the world's most dangerous and life-threatening "trick."

GOOGLE GUIDE

Chapter 4: It's a Jungle Out There

For more on this subject, try these:

"Brother, Can You Spare a Dime," by Bing Crosby. (song).
Find title at YouTube: http://www.youtube.com/

"National Recovery Administration - NRA Promo -1933." (MGM film). http://www.archive.org/details/National1933/

"Memoirs of a Sandlot Kid," by Gordon Greb, Dec. 5, 2005. (column).
http://www.thecolumnists.com/greb/greb16.html

For a longer listing, go to the book's web site:

Google Brain Book: http://googlebrainbook.blogspot.com/

Chapter 5

Goodbye, Old Man Depression

*There were times when my pants were so thin I could sit
on a dime and know if it was heads or tails.*

——Spencer Tracy (1900-1967)

I believe that to understand a Great Depression, every political
candidate needs to know how it feels to be down and out. He or she
needs to be well trained in the trenches to understand what happens in
social catastrophes.

What every man and woman in public office needs is a grass roots
understanding of what it feels like to be unemployed, hungry, and
without a home. It's to provide that kind of preparation for war that
the military assigns every recruit or draftee to a realistic basic training
course. With America and world in trouble again after the stock market
crashed again in the fall of 2008, we, the people, have put a new man
in the White House to figure out what to do. Does anyone today really
have enough experience to know what to do?

Since President Barack Obama now has this responsibility, I feel
we should implement FDR's request of long ago that "We Do Our
Part" in the national recovery effort. This means, of course, I plan to
go to Washington, D.C. to help the President. Naturally I'll want to
talk to him about our dogs and missing memoirs, but then I have
some great ideas to tell him on how we can improve our representative
democracy.

Knowing he is smart and constantly looking for new ideas, I'm positive that he will be interested in the following proposal because it's really quite simple. Let me tell you what will vastly improve policy making in our country in one sentence:

> *There shall be a new law, enacted by Congress and signed by the President, the purpose of which shall be to better qualify candidates for office in the federal government, by establishing a School of Hard Knocks,*
>
> *To teach and/or simulate the actual conditions experienced by individuals and families going through severe economic distress, such as a Great Depression, Joblessness, Homelessness or its equivalency,*
>
> *That if taken voluntarily, candidates seeking election to office will prove to constituents their serious desire to understand the plight and needs of those less well off than themselves, and know what to do about it by experiencing their needs themselves.*

Until our governmental representatives get this kind of practical knowledge, the only other avenue to the truth for them is to follow the advice given doctoral students in graduate school—go to original sources. Anyone can learn how a Hard Knocks School would function by simply volunteering at any homeless shelter, center for the poor, or kitchen for the needy near where one lives. That's where these lessons begin.

After the Big Crash of 1929, my brother and I were thrown into that kind of school. We understood its effects not only from what was happening to us but also from what we saw on the screen at our local movie theaters. We also read headline after headline in the *Oakland Tribune* about businesses closing, banks failing, and factories laying off workers.

My father was among those affected. He lost both his tire shop and our home. The Great Depression came down on us like a bomb. My young parents, Walter and Irene Greb, who were both thirty-four years old at the time, couldn't believe what was happening. As my dad remarked later, "It hit us like a ton of bricks and there was nobody to help us." My parents had always been self-reliant but now they were reeling from forces they couldn't understand. It's no wonder they couldn't figure it out.

With millions out of work, facing an uncertain future, and nowhere to turn, the tragedy of the early 1930s played no favorites. The sudden downturn hit every segment of society alike—employers and employees, national brands and local craftsmen, major retailers and local merchants. We saw photographs of hungry men in long breadlines in newspapers. We witnessed newsreels showing dairy farmers dumping huge cans of fresh milk into the streets, because too few people could afford to buy what they were producing.

As anger spread across the country, people began asking themselves, why couldn't something be done? Americans of the early 1930s had no unemployment insurance, housing allowances, or Social Security checks. There was no program to put the unemployed back to work, although several would come into effect as soon as President Franklin D. Roosevelt took office.

Without a job in 1930, my father couldn't keep up the monthly payments on our home. Our family faced eviction until loan officers realized the real estate market was dead and they had no new buyers. Since they couldn't sell, the bank agreed to let us stay on the property as long as we paid rent. They wanted $20 per month. My parents had no choice, agreed to the terms, but were thinking to themselves, "Where is our next dollar coming from?" A banker and real estate broker connected to our East Bay property both committed suicide.

During the depth of the depression, jobs were few and far between. My dad left our home every day, looking for work. Despite all of their worries, my parents tried very hard not to burden us children. No matter how much they must have worried inwardly Mom and Pop always tried to be cheerful and uncomplaining. Although my brother and I were young, we didn't have to guess to know what was going on. We knew we were poor but hated to think so.

Whenever Pop came home to tell us he had found a new part-time job, it was a happy moment in our family. Whatever each job paid, my mother tried to squirrel away extra nickels and dimes in the cupboard for an emergency. She always kept something hidden away for our household budget. The thought of my brother and I ever stealing from her kitty never entered out minds.

Each morning my dad got up early, set out looking for work, and took every offer made. As long as he remained healthy he said, "I'll take any job handed me." He became a newspaper delivery boy, an ice truck driver, and a service station operator, and never quit trying. Anything to keep us going. None of it amounted to a living wage but every little bit helped. At one time our family income dropped to $40 per month. With half going for rent, my folks nearly hit bottom. Yet somehow they managed.

Our meals at home were simple. For supper Mom gave us hamburger patties that she breaded to last longer, mashed potatoes, gravy, and a helping of peas, carrots, or vegetables in season. She never failed to serve fish on Fridays. We kids got milk and the adults, coffee. While dessert was only on special occasions, everything on the table was affordable, nourishing, and chosen to sustain the health of a hardworking husband and her two boys.

What kept us going was the stubborn refusal of my parents to give up. When no job openings had turned up, what were they supposed to do? On one such an occasion, I inadvertently touched a raw nerve in my father, whose feelings of self-worth required that he never show an ounce of weakness to others. Innocently I excitedly came home from school to tell my dad, "Hey, Pop, I just found out some great news! A kid told me where there's a church giving away free boxes of food and all we have to do is go there and get it."

Suddenly dropping his newspaper and rising to his feet, he addressed me with great seriousness, saying, "Son, I never want to hear you say anything like that to me again! As long as your father has strong arms and legs, I am perfectly capable of feeding this family myself. We are not taking charity from anyone."

Because he could play the guitar, banjo, and violin, my dad asked some friends to join him in organizing a four-piece hillbilly band to play for hire. It became known as *Walt's Hay Bailers*, named by my mother. At night in bed I could hear Pop's fiddle, Slim's percussion, Whitey's guitar, and Herb's bass violin, practicing into the night. I'd hear numbers like *She'll be Coming 'Round the Mountain, Three Little Words,* and *It Ain't Gonna Rain No More, No More* as they rehearsed for their next performance. My dad's band got dates to play at large dances or small private homes.

Occasionally *Walt's Hay Bailers* appeared at movie theatres, fairs, and radio stations. One time I took the stage with him at the Capitol Theater in an amateur contest, dressed in my Tom Mix cowboy outfit with a violin tucked under my arm. We took first prize doing *They Cut Down the Old Pine Tree* and *The Old Spinning Wheel*. I sawed away with my bow and my father strummed the guitar.

Mom's frugality was amazing. By careful budgeting, my mother could save enough nickels and dimes in a sugar bowl to tide us over when nothing was coming in. How my mother became so adept at finding ways to feed her family on such a slim budget I'll never know. The economics department at the University of California should have awarded her an honorary degree. She had been an English literature major at San Jose Normal School (now San Jose State University) when she was a young woman but now she was a self-taught home economist.

My mother couldn't afford to buy us new shoes or get any resoled. So she fitted pieces of cardboard inside our tattered shoes and sent us off with the worn spots covered. This, however, was a temporary fix that didn't last. By afternoon my artificial cardboard soles had worn through and I could feel the cold pavement against my stocking feet. Always frugal she never spent money for postage stamps to pay the bills. She walked the five to ten blocks to pay the water, gas, and electric bills in person at local offices. She bought groceries at places offering good value for money, usually at Piggly Wiggly or family-owned grocery stores around Havenscourt and Seminary avenues.

At night or when they were alone, I often heard my parents exchanging anxious worries behind closed doors about where the next dollar was coming from. I could catch much of their whispered conversations even though their bedroom door was shut. While this concerned my brother and me, my folks never knew it. They tried to conceal the strain to protect us. Times were definitely tough when your parents can't spare you a nickel or a dime to spend on candy, ice cream, or chewing gum.

Though money was scarce and my mother had to economize everyway she could, she never skimped on feeding her family, saying,

"Never be ashamed of being poor if your clothes are clean and you work for an honest dollar."

Happy days returned to America the day we heard FDR's startling inaugural address on March 4, 1933. Despite the sprinkling of rain that fell on the nation's capital, Roosevelt's voice conveyed confidence and hope to the entire nation, when he said clearly and firmly, "Only a foolish optimist can deny the dark realities of the moment ... Our greatest primary task is to put people to work."

Despite the pain of heavy metal supports wrapped around his crippled legs, which none of us were aware of at the time, Roosevelt pulled himself up to his feet and was a man determined to bring the whole nation to its feet along with him. Roosevelt challenged people to be brave, not be disheartened by fear, assuring them he intended to act on their behalf.

Roosevelt's assessment of the nation's problems raised our spirits. What the Greb family needed was a steady job for father as soon as possible—as did millions of families like us—a steady, good wage-paying job. FDR gave the unemployed confidence that somehow this would happen. That was the chief hope of my parents when they cast their ballots for him that last November.

My dad smiled at the conclusion of the speech, saying, "I think we've finally got the right man in the White House." Congress acted quickly to turn FDR's programs into law, passing an amazing fifteen pieces of legislation in less than one hundred days. But many of the New Deal program benefits took time to reach us in 1933.

What Roosevelt's New Deal finally did arrive in Oakland, California, my father jumped at the chance for a job with the Public Works Administration (PWA), which paid about $40 a month. Pop felt no shame joining this special, government-sponsored project because he would work for every cent he was being paid. It was not a handout. One time he was given the task of clearing brush and debris along a riverbed, which gave him a bad case of poison oak afterward. It's a cruel joke to say my dad had been reduced to scratching for a living.

When the economy picked up, one of the big Oakland construction companies started hiring men to dig a highway tunnel through the East Bay hills to the Walnut Creek area, the Caldecott Tunnel. My Dad worked for months with pneumatic drills, shovels, and heavy equipment till it was finished. Another part-time position that he especially liked was operating a small switch steam engine at a steel plant in Alameda. But the next job he took almost claimed his life, even though it seemed routine when he first signed on to do it.

Employed to help a major contractor build a new men's gymnasium on the campus of the University of California, Pop stepped aside to let another man go ahead of him up a ramp. Since the unfinished structure rose from two to three stories in height, some of the men had to push wheelbarrows of cement over wooden planks laid across the top floor and my dad was one of them. On reaching the highest level on one of these trips, a board suddenly slipped, gave way, and hurled the worker ahead of my father three floors down to his death.

When shouts of the accident first reached other men, some thought they heard, "Greb's been killed" when actually witnesses had shouted that "Fred's been killed." It's good that false report never reached my mother before it was scotched. A still riskier job was to come later and again he was lucky.

The contractor building the Oakland-San Francisco Bay Bridge needed experienced men to work at great heights and my dad needed a paycheck. Willing to tackle anything, he told the job interviewer when asked about his experience, "Have I ever done high construction work? Sure, plenty of experience. That's me." So he got the job.

The day he climbed the bridge structure and tried balancing himself on the narrow beams, the more experienced men immediately spotted him as an unsteady amateur. When the boss realized Greb would likely fall into San Francisco Bay if he didn't do something, he decided on the spot to make him the timekeeper. This put my dad in a little wooden house half-way up the side of the bridge, but every day he had to climb up there. Years later he would laugh, saying, "If you took a look at the iron rungs up there today, you'd still find my finger prints in the metal because I was holding on so hard."

I look back today in admiration at how my parents kept up their psychological strength and dignity. They tried to remain calm and caring despite adversity. My young brother and I often rebelled over trivial demands they made on our young lives, never quite understanding why we had to go to bed early, eat all the food on our plates, or take castor oil for an illness. But we did what we were told.

Deep down we knew it must be for our own benefit. They taught us to be honest, loyal, courteous, obedient, diligent, and so forth. They were moral values that our schools and churches reinforced as well as our relatives and neighbors. But the most memorable piece of advice from my father was his admonition to "think for yourself and never let someone else do your thinking for you." He said a man has to be tough, stand up for himself, and not let anybody push him around.

Roosevelt was more than a great president—he was a great teacher who could explain complicated problems plainly and simply. You felt he was talking to you personally when he went on the radio. On the evening he was to broadcast one of his "Fireside Chats," you could walk down the street and hear his voice coming out the windows of nearly every home. No matter where they were or what they were doing, people stopped everything to hear what Roosevelt had to say.

Although the Great Depression is long gone and relegated to the history books, my memory of those days is still strong, and I still sympathize with people today who are facing similar situations. That's why we have a continuing need for more leaders with empathy for those less fortunate than themselves. That's why I'm advocating the creation of a School of Hard Knocks so that future politicians can deal swiftly and competently with social and economic disasters and protect the people it hits hardest. Doing this would be an important step toward achieving what the founding fathers of our republic had intended—to "promote the general Welfare, and secure the Blessings of Liberty to ourselves and to our own Posterity...."

GOOGLE GUIDE

Chapter 5: Goodbye, Old Man Depression

For more on this subject, try these:

"Happy Days Are Here Again" by Ben Salving and the Crooners. (song). Find title at YouTube: http://www.youtube.com/

"FDR–The Man Who Changed America" (film). http://www.youtube.com/watch?v=Ew2j3P0OJeg&feature=fvw/

"Goodbye, Old Man Depression," by Gordon Greb. (column). http://www.thecolumnists.com/greb/greb23.html/

For a longer listing, go to the book's web site:

Google Brain Book: http://googlebrainbook.blogspot.com/

Chapter 6

Pick Yourself Up

Thrusting my nose firmly between his teeth, I threw him heavily to the ground on top of me.

——Mark Twain (1835-1910)

A word of advice to fellow earthlings and especially to all young hopefuls out there eager to be successful: your goal in life should be to figure out how to be big! Think about it and you'll know it's true.

First, everyone is born little. Big people look down at you, talk down to you, pick you up, and put you down, and maybe carry you about until you fuss too much. They seem to be absolutely in charge of everything that happens when you're small. You seem absolutely helpless, bewildered, and completely at the mercy of all the big people looking down at you from up above. They're in charge and there's nothing you can do about it. Well, not exactly! Your little brain quickly learns something.

Second, you learn what to do to become big! It's simply that you find out that whenever you have a big need of something, you huff and puff to become huge in the eyes and ears of the beholder! You tighten up your vocal chords and let out a series of big, long, noises! Moreover you keep on making this terrible noise to inform the whole darn universe that you want something and want it now! In my experience and yours, too, I can imagine you either got instant results or you didn't stop yelling to high heaven until you got what you needed—a bottle of warm milk or your nappy changed.

This is when the brain kicks in and you learn how to use what's on top of your spinal column. It's the start of what you'll do for the rest of your natural life. You and I learn from infancy that you need to find ways to deal with everything big or it will forever dominate you. But being big is only part of the answer. There's more than aspiring to huge physical size.

Since animal bigness is power that can be abused, you'll need to recognize that there are other forces besides bigness, which, believe it or not, little people can use to manipulate the truly big monsters. We've learned much of that from the tales we've heard from the brothers Grimm, Aesop, and Hans Christian Anderson. They're the lessons of the *Ugly Duckling, Thumbelina, Cinderella, Little Red Riding Hood,* and the *Three Little Pigs.*

It's what you experience over and over again interacting with other people. If you want to become a real boy, as the story of *Pinocchio* goes, you need to wake up and start using your brain. Thus it's time that you realized, dear reader, that you are constantly writing the story of your own life in your book of time, experimenting constantly on how to become big. Hopefully you'll write down what you've learned for young people to read, or at least tell them in some fashion what they need to know. It's never too late.

Today your memories can be preserved in diaries, typewritten stories, still photos, motion picture film, tape recordings, digital discs, computer hard drives, or personal web sites. Believe it or not, extraordinary experiences aren't the monopoly of big people. We all have them from the moment of our birth. One of the assignments I've given students in writing classes has been to step outside the classroom to interview the first person they meet. I guarantee whoever they accidentally encounter will have a great story to tell.

Before I was old enough for kindergarten, I stood on the front porch of our Oakland home and asked the kids on the way to school, "Do you want to fight?" Lucky for me none of them accepted my challenge, choosing to pass me by, perhaps wondering what was wrong with that crazy little kid.

By the time I learned that tough talk too easily led to fist fights, I had been in too many of them. Often I've wondered why I'd acquired that aggressive persona? Could it have been the movies? My Dad loved movies of all kinds. So he took me to see them at a very early age, never realizing that some of them might have strong and unanticipated influences on his son from what was being shown on the screen.

We went in the evening to our neighborhood Capitol Theater while Mom stayed home with the baby. I ran to get into Pop's car because I loved going to the movies. This was before the talkies. A booming pipe organ set the mood for silent films like those starring Charlie Chaplin in *The Gold Rush* or Harold Lloyd in *Safety Last*. We sat there enthralled by the loud, rippling sounds of the theater's pipe organist, who often played variations from the classics. So you can imagine what ideas got into my head as a kid with my eyes glued to war hero John Gilbert braving the bombs and bullets in *The Big Parade* and a swashbuckling Douglas Fairbanks swinging his sword in the role of *Zorro*.

Movies taught that to be a real man, you had to stand up and fight. That's what cowboy heroes did in westerns starring Bronco Billy Anderson, William S. Hart, and Tom Mix. In each of them I saw lots of knockdown, drag-out fighting in barroom brawls, which told my little brain that you always had to fight with your fists when bullies challenged your rights. So I began challenging every kid who passed my house when barely four years old.

While Pop taught me to stand up for myself, I don't believe my father ever struck another man with his fists except in the army. For a brief period in the First World War, he boxed overseas in France for the entertainment of soldiers but never professionally. However, there was a famous New York boxer by the name of Harry Greb, who twice became a world champion in the 1920s. In the ring for 299 fights in a 13-year career, Harry Greb was a major sports world personality for his time, considered by sports writers of his era to be one of the greatest fighters of all time. With an unorthodox windmill boxing style against opponents, he took both the middleweight and light heavyweight crowns. Due to this man's fame, my father soon found himself nicknamed "Harry Greb" by men he worked with, and the psychological impact of that name probably helped dampen more than one potential opponent's temper in tense situations.

The day I learned that fisticuffs weren't the only way to solve a problem came when I was a bit older. It happened when Pop was speeding down Foothill Boulevard in our fancy Graham Page automobile and not noticing how fast he was driving. Seated beside my dad in front, I easily observed what personality and language can accomplish as Pop persuaded the motorcycle cop not to give him a ticket. Pop could be like an Irishman who had kissed the Blarney Stone when he wanted to. And he could disarm an opponent with persuasion as easily as with threats of open violence.

Nevertheless I grew up believing that I had to be strong, brave, and ready to do battle for what was right, which ended up giving me several black eyes and bloody noses. Half the time I took on kids older, bigger, and stronger than I because a bully would be picking on my younger brother or some other little kid. If the cause seemed right, I felt an obligation, win or lose, to protect those who needed it.

As an undersized, skinny kid, in need of glasses for poor eyesight, I ought not to have been fighting at all. One time ten-year old Ray Hutchinson, who lived a few blocks away, caught me going home on my roller skates and started pounding away. It must have been a funny sight, because every time I tried to get up, he quickly knocked me down. But no matter who won each encounter, we soon forget about it afterward and were friends.

The most serious incident in my young pugilistic career came during my last term at Whittier Grammar School in the sixth grade. I began arguing with classmate Clarence Martin over a baseball game at recess because he had grabbed the bat and shoved me aside, insisting it was his turn at the plate. The school bell rang, we argued on our way into the building, and finally came to blows.

A male Whittier Grammar School teacher caught both of us scrapping like a couple of wildcats in the hallway, grabbed us by our ears, and hauled us into the principal's office. Unable to figure out which of one of us had started the skirmish, the school's chief administrator applied what seemed the most appropriate action and punished us both.

Marching us into his office individually, he turned each of us over his knee and gave our bottoms a good whacking with a leather strap. The humility was worse than the pain. Also I feared what would come next. After the principal sent word to my parents, I dreaded what my own dad would do and was surprised when he let me go with a stern warning to think twice before letting it happen again.

Defending little kids like my brother—making sure they weren't picked upon by the older boys—got me into plenty of scraps as it was the culture I knew growing up during the Great Depression. Kids were imitating what happened to their elders. As we grew older we were not sheltered from current events.

In the summer of 1934, all the papers on the newsstands carried stories and photos of the police beating up men on the streets of San Francisco during what was called a General Strike—a call for all workers to walk off their jobs. As the strikers assembled, the city called out the police, and violence ensued. We kids saw it, heard our parents talk about it, and knew sometimes fighting was the only thing left to do. But unlike Hollywood's version of the *Dead End Kids*, none of us on 64th Avenue became young toughs willing to break the law. As far as I can remember none of the kids I knew engaged in shoplifting, stealing, or thievery, which would have had us arrested. But Oakland kids weren't all puritanical. On New Year's Day 1930, someone burned down Fremont High School and not long afterward, another fire of unknown origin wrecked havoc at Lockwood Junior High.

If you've ever been hit in the eye in a fistfight (which happens to boys growing up), you would have experienced a flash of sudden and terrific pain no matter how hard the impact. Each time that happened to me, I felt like the blow did not come from another human being but from something invented by Mother Nature—the force of gravity. On one occasion, the strength of that impact was strong enough to cause me to lose consciousness. It sent me into a pit of pitch darkness, which fortunately lasted for only a short time and had me gasping for air when recovery began. It took only a few seconds or perhaps minutes before I was able to open my eyes to blurred vision and confused sounds. Then my bewildered mind began trying to orient itself and figure out what happened.

When my confusion abated, my brain finally realized I had fallen from a high place and struck something solid coming down. My mind took hold and started to adjust itself to the predicament and I immediately uttered a small silent cry for help. I'd been climbing among the high rafters of the barn on my grandmother's farm, lost my grip, and fallen head first onto a big oil drum, which opened the back of my skull and left me dazed and bleeding.

When I staggered up the stairs and through the door into the house, it was on my parent's thirteenth wedding anniversary. They stared in disbelief at their twelve-year old son bleeding from the back of the head, bleary-eyed, and nearly ready to pass out. My mother quickly found a towel to wrap around my head, and my father picked me up, hurried me into his car, and drove me to the doctor's office, where the wound was examined, sewn up, and bandaged. On returning home I was put to bed, told to rest, and instructed to let nature to take its course. Despite the fact my head was throbbing and aching painfully, I dropped off to a deep sleep the moment it hit the pillow.

When sufficiently improved to return to school, I became an object of curiosity among my classmates when I showed up with my head wrapped up in turban-like bandages. It was awful being forced to appear in the public this way, having everyone starring strangely at me, and I could hardly wait till I was a normal kid again. When that day finally arrived, I was totally unaware of its after effects, which seemed unimportant at the time. But the consequences should not have been so casually dismissed. That accident probably changed the rest of my life. Although it could have killed me instantly, that hard blow merely halted momentarily my steady progress toward becoming a full-fledged adult. While it left a deep scar beneath the hair on the back of my neck and was visible for years after leaving the barbershop, I never realized until recently what it had done.

Since it happened when I was very young and my recovery appeared normal, I quickly ignored this childhood event and never thought of it again unless someone asked how I got the scar on my head. Now I think it did more than crack my skull and cause physical pain—it gave me some kind of shock treatment, which in some wonderful way caused me to see my life and the world around me differently. Somehow it stopped my going in one direction and sent me in another. It caused me to pause. It possibly gave me time to think. And in so doing made me focus on the "now" and what I was doing about it. Adults would say, "That boy at last is settling down."

GOOGLE GUIDE

Chapter 6: Pick Yourself Up

For more on this subject, try these:

"Pick Yourself Up – Swing Time (1936)," by Fred Astaire and Ginger Rogers. (song). Time: 2:10 min. Find title at YouTube: http://www.youtube.com/

"Bullets or Ballots (1936). (movie trailer).
Find title at YouTube: http://www.youtube.com/

"The Brown Bomber vs. Hitler's Pride," by Stan Isaacs. (column).
http://www.thecolumnists.com/isaacs/isaacs3B05.html/

For a longer listing, go to the book's web site:

Google Brain Book: http://googlebrainbook.blogspot.com/

Chapter 7

Who's Afraid of the Big Bad Wolf?

Money is better than poverty, if only for financial reasons.

——Woody Allen (1935-)

When President Roosevelt was trying hard to get us out of the Great Depression, he got unanticipated help from an unexpected source—a musical show of singing and dancing that lifted the spirits of everyone who saw it. It wasn't a big stage production by Florence Ziegfeld, a three-ring circus by Barnum & Bailey, or a visual display of feminine charms choreographed by Busby Berkeley in a new Hollywood feature. It was an eight-minute movie—a color cartoon called the *Three Little Pigs* that was destined to win an Academy Award.

When audiences saw it for the first time in New York City on May 27, 1933, at the film's premiere, it was hardly one hundred days after the inauguration of the new president. Carefully crafted by Walt Disney and his animators at their Hyperion Studios in Hollywood, it became a sensation when audiences began seeing it in cities and towns not only in America but also around the world. Screened for the first time at the Radio City Music Hall, its effect was magical and its timing couldn't have been better.

At his March 4th inauguration Roosevelt's told a depressed country not to be afraid. Because the country's morale had hit rock bottom and FDR needed all the help he could get to restore people's confidence, that's exactly what began to happen after more and more people began seeing Disney's Technicolor *Three Little Pigs*. Starting a month after the inauguration, people coming out of theaters were whistling and singing the theme song they'd just heard—"Who's Afraid of the Big Bad Wolf?" Thanks to radio stations playing it from coast to coast, there was hardly anyone in America (whose population was 120 million, according to the 1930 census) who hadn't heard the song before 1933 was over.

That Christmas those with children living in San Francisco's East Bay flocked to see the window display of the Dollar Store in downtown Oakland—a scene of one Little Pig busy building a brick house, while the other Two Little Pigs were dancing around their huts completely unaware of the Big Bad Wolf, whose movements back and forth showed he was lurking dangerously near. We watched in fascination as sound amplifiers played the song over and over, "Who's Afraid of the Big Bad Wolf?" to the crowds gathered in front of the downtown store.

When my family—my father, mother, brother and I—saw the movie of the *Three Little Pigs* for the first time in the fall of 1933 at a little neighborhood theater in Alameda, we looked at each other in astonishment. What we had seen on the screen was amazing—a children's' fairy tale brought to life in such an intriguing and delightful way. Our eyes had been dazzled by color, our ears by music, and our common sense challenged by the lifelike characters that danced and sang like ordinary human beings.

We stared in disbelief watching three lively little pigs that were so child-like you wanted to almost hug and kiss them. We sat on the edge of our seats anxious to make sure they'd actually escape those terrible teeth of that drooling and black-eyed monster, the big bad wolf. This was not simply our reaction as children. It was how it left both of my parents, who were equally amazed.

When the cartoon ended, we had been in the theater for over two hours. But my mother hardly hesitated a moment before asking the question, "Do you want to stay to see that cartoon again?" We knew this would mean sitting through the long black-and-white feature film a second time but fairly shouted our unanimous consent, "Yes! We want to stay to see it again!" I was twelve years old. My brother was eight. My parents were both thirty-eight.

The next day I wrote a fan letter to Walt Disney. First, to thank him for all of his wonderful cartoons. Second, to tell him I was a twelve-year old boy hoping to work for him as a cartoonist when I grew up.

Third, to present him with my own cartoon—a penciled sketch of my imagined reaction of Mickey Mouse to this latest Silly Symphony color cartoon. My drawing showed huge crowds pushing and shoving to get into a theatre where the marquee read, "Now Playing—Three Little Pigs." But it also showed a downhearted Mickey Mouse, walking down a side alley with his hands pushed deep into his pockets, saying, "Gosh, I hope they don't forget about me."

Walt Disney not only replied but thanked me for my letter and the cartoon about Mickey Mouse, assuring me, "Mickey Mouse isn't all sad, though, because we have the jolliest stories planned for him that will take him gaily along until next Christmas time." Telling me to hold fast to my ambition to become a Disney artist, I was told another package was coming to me in the mail. What I got was an original, hand-colored drawing of Mickey Mouse. He was standing on a tree stump leading the three little pigs, who were playing musical instruments and singing a song shown in a big balloon as, "Best Wishes to Gordon Greb." The cartoon was signed below by the man himself, "Sincerely, Walt Disney."

Inspired by Disney, I survived the Great Depression by selling my cartoons to newspapers and magazines from grammar school through high school. Yes, I credit Disney for having inspired me to do it because he knew how to pick and judge talent. He looked for new ideas constantly and was deeply involved every step of the way in each of his early productions. After Disney found the "Three Little Pigs" story in Andrew Lang's *Green Fairy* book, he circulated a note to his staff, saying that these "little pig characters look as if they would work up very cute" and advocating that the animators strive to give them real personalities.

What helped make the *Three Little Pigs* a success was Disney's foresight and adaptability to new technology. In order to get exclusive rights to a new color processing system in his animated cartoons, Walt signed a three-year contract with Technicolor. His brother Roy, the business manager, thought it too risky. But perceptive and creative Walt took the gamble anyway, finally producing a great movie with Burt Gillett, director; Frank Churchill, music composer; Ted Sears, lyricist; Pinto Colvig, singer of the theme song; and animators Dick Lundy, Norm Ferguson, Art Babbitt, and Fred Moore.

For years I had only my own memory of the movie to cherish until shopping one day for gifts for my young grandchildren in Toys 'R Us. There I found Disney's *Three Little Pigs* on videotape, which gave me a chance to see it again for the first time in more than seventy-five years. Seeing it again confirms my belief it was a masterpiece.

You must see the *Three Little Pigs* to understand why I consider it one of Walt Disney's greatest achievements. The *Three Little Pigs* is a perfect example of Walt Disney's genius. It's why he ended up winning 32 Academy Awards in his lifetime, more than any other single individual in the history of Hollywood. And also why he remained true to the little mouse that got him started in the first place.

Seeing the film again told me I that had worried needlessly over the possibility that Walt Disney would ever forget about his little mouse. At the beginning of the movie, Disney made sure who got star billing, with the title reading: "Mickey Mouse presents Walt Disney's Silly Symphony—*Three Little Pigs*." Look at who got star billing!

Inspired by Disney I began getting my cartoons published on the children's page of the city's two daily newspapers, the *Oakland Tribune* and *Oakland Post Enquirer*. I also began publishing my own newspaper called *The Katz Meow* with the help of my friend Jack Corbett. We sold and distributed our little weekly at Frick Junior High and Lockwood Junior High. At the peak of its success, the May Company of Los Angeles set up an exhibit at its downtown store to show that two boys were able to publish a newspaper using its printing supplies.

I also advertised our newspaper by entering the national Soap Box Derby race, driving a car named *The Katz Meow* down the steep hill of 35th Avenue in Oakland one summer, but by coming in last, I missed a chance to publicize it nationally before newsreel cameras at Akron, Ohio, in the finals.

Going to downtown Oakland by car one time with my father, I saw empty stores along the way, factory buildings closed, doors locked, and windows smashed. Old Man Depression constantly knocked on to our own front door as strangers tried to sell us something. Before long, I, too, was doing the same, canvassing the neighborhood to sell magazines, raffle tickets, or wreathes during Christmas season.

To get any sweets, my brother and I had to earn our own money. One of the ways I picked up some small change was going from house to house, peddling the *Saturday Evening Post, Liberty* and *Ladies Home Journal*. Each week as new issues came out, I'd get the new copies delivered to our front door, cut the twine, and stuff them in my bag, before making my rounds to customers. I still remember the pungent smell of new printer's ink and thrill it gave me to be the very first person to open the pages of each issue. The retail price of the *Saturday Evening Post* was five cents and my share was one and one-half cents.

With so many parents out of work—one out of four families across America—it was easy to figure out who were suffering the most. You'd know by how many of your school pals were scrambling for part-time jobs and accepting what was offered no matter how little it paid. Candy bars cost a nickel, movies a dime, and a good restaurant lunch, twenty-five cents. If you could face taking "no" for an answer and having doors slammed in your face, you'd walk for hours going house to house, offering to cut lawns, sell magazines, or run errands. Some of our sales pitches worked, others didn't. Trying to sell old periodicals, bags of marbles, or windup toys to passersby from a wagon was one of my bright entrepreneurial ideas, but it merely gave me a chance to watch the world go by without making a single sale.

The sound that buoyed our hopes on 64th Avenue anytime in the early 1930s was hearing the words "any rags, bottles, sacks" sung out by an old Italian seated on a horse-drawn wagon who was urging his animal down the street. Since my mother saved everything, saying, "We may have use for this someday," our storage bins were always full of stuff, and she welcomed the ragman as a rare opportunity to turn it into money right at our doorstep.

When the ragman's call rang out, I'd run out into the street to stop the wagon, fetch my mother, and watch how she would sell nearly everything in the nooks and crannies of the garage—old gunny sacks, empty bottles, yellowed newspapers, and magazines, rusty tools, broken clocks, and old chunks of iron. We didn't call it recycling in those days but that's what it was.

What I liked hearing best in those days was the voice of my next-door neighbor Mrs. Hurst calling me to go on an errand. A cheerful, middle-aged woman, she always predicted, "Gordon, someday you're going to be president." Mrs. Hurst was well off because her husband was "working steady" as a carpenter for the Oakland-San Francisco

Ferry Company. She would pay me a nickel to run to the store for a pound of sugar, can of beans, or bottle of milk. She would have me buy a pound of hamburger for ten cents or a loaf of bread for eight cents. On the way home I'd take a detour to stop off at Mr. Norton's candy store on Foothill Boulevard, opposite Frick school, to spend what I'd earned by choosing a five-cent candy bar, a *Snickers, Milky Way,* or *Hershey.*

Radio made a big effort to get our attention in the thirties. Since kids were attracted to the children's hour in the late afternoon, broadcasters tried selling them products like *Wheaties* or *Ovaltine.* Consequently if we weren't playing baseball, riding our bikes, or hunting for creepy crawly things in the creek, you'd find us at home listening to the radio programs like *Tarzan, Lord of the Jungle; Jack Armstrong, the All American Boy;* or *"Little Orphan Annie.*

So it's no wonder that an *Oakland Tribune* story caught my attention when it said, "School Radio Class Offered" and I decided to go. Arriving early, I found myself the only kid in attendance because it was an evening class for adults. Highly embarrassed for being out of place, I headed for the door as soon as the bell rang and never went back. But it left me wondering, "What would it be like to be on the radio?"

Cartooning led me into doing comic strips, such as "Fishy Tales" and "Squirrel Town" which the Oakland papers carried. Then I began drawing fighter planes, showing the brave pilots of the First World War flying Spads and Campbells in dogfights with the Fokker D7s of the enemy. Little did I know that forming my own club called the "Dare Devil Aces" (which, by the way, was the name of an illustrated pulp fiction magazine) would take me into radio.

One day in early 1934, I entered my fighter plane drawings in a radio contest advertised by *Rusty, the Boy Aviator,* which I heard at 5:15 every weekday afternoon over station KTAB in Oakland. Much to my surprise I won the contest and was invited to come to its Oakland radio studios to be interviewed on Rusty's special Saturday morning variety show, the "Jamboree."

Invited to return the following week, I brought along a short skit called, "The Adventures of Gordon and Jack," written in collaboration with my twelve-year old friend Jack Corbett, which the producer liked. Since Rusty was sponsored by Dr. Korley's So Clean Toothpaste, I managed to work in a plug for the sponsor in each of our weekly episodes. The producer liked it so much he said we should do it each Saturday morning.

Then a surprising thing happened. After we'd finished doing one of those "Gordon and Jack" skits on the little Saturday morning show, the producer noticed my voice was nearly identical to the kid who played Rusty. Since the youngster playing the part was leaving to accept a more lucrative offer from NBC, the show needed a young actor to replace him and the producer asked me whether I wanted to do it.

"Sure," I said. "But what about school? I don't get out of school till 3:15 every afternoon."

"No problem" he said. "You'll still have two hours to reach the Oakland studios by bus and have plenty of time to rehearse before we hit the air at 5:15."

Whatever adventures awaited me on the radio, they were cut short. Although Rusty had found a way to escape crocodiles in the Amazon, plane crashes in the Andes, and savages of Africa, it was a measles bug that finally brought his high-flying ambitions down to earth in the end. With nobody to replace me on a show that was live, the exciting adventures of *Rusty, Boy Aviator* went off the air and I became just a plain ordinary kid again.

But my dream of taking my first airplane ride was realized. Thanks to building and flying a winning model airplane, I won one of the prizes—a chance to fly aboard a Varney Speedline passenger plane. The few kids lucky enough to have been chosen met at Alameda airport, walked out onto the flying field, and climbed the steps into the cabin. About nine of us found our seats in this single-engine monoplane and took a twenty-minute ride over the San Francisco Bay Area, looking down at Oakland-San Francisco Bay Bridge as it was being built. Walter T. Varney, the airline's owner, used this promotion to prove to people that it was safe to fly. He seemed to have succeeded since Varney Speed Lines became Continental Airlines in 1937.

Sometimes my proud and self-reliant family was forced to sell what we really loved out of sheer necessity. I first began to notice this happening when things began disappearing from our house. For example, we had a lovely upright player piano on which I was trying to learn how to play. My fondest memory is being at the piano keyboard trying to compose a new song and the disappointment when it didn't turn out right. With quiet care, my mother would say, "Doesn't your new song sound a lot like 'My Bonnie Lies Over the Ocean'?" In frustration over being unable to compose something new, I blurted out, "I think they've used up all the notes" and left the piano for good. If I had any second thoughts about trying to compose music, that quickly ended them.

The day I came home from school and I saw our lovely player piano was gone was a terrible shock. What remained was a huge empty space in the corner of our living room. Not having a piano in our house would be unheard of. I can remember seeing them in nearly all the neighborhood homes I visited. Ours was there when Pop rehearsed with his hillbilly band and when my brother Wallace and I wanted to generate our own music using piano rolls. The Aeolian Company pianola was easy to operate. All a person had to do was to find the song you wanted on a roll, insert it into the piano slot, and start pumping the foot pedal to activate the piano keyboard and hear the music.

Losing the piano was the beginning of the realization that my folks were being forced to sell valuable keepsakes and possessions to raise money to live on—the epitome being reached when my father had to pawn his expensive, gold railroad watch in order to pay the bills. Luckily I had my Mickey Mouse pocket watch to loan him when the railroad called him back to work, which gave him a timepiece until he could retrieve his own. That's how you survive a Great Depression. With Mickey Mouse in your pocket, who's afraid of the big bad wolf?

GOOGLE GUIDE

Chapter 7: Who's Afraid of the Big Bad Wolf?

For more on this subject, try these:

"Who's Afraid of the Big, Bad Wolf?" (song).
Find title at YouTube: http://www.youtube.com/

Newsreel: "All-American Soap Box Derby (1936)." (newsreel).
Find title at YouTube: http://www.youtube.com/

"San Francisco General Strike Newsreel 1/2 (1934)." (newsreel).
Find title at YouTube: http://www.youtube.com/

For a longer listing, go to the book's web site:

Google Brain Book: http://googlebrainbook.blogspot.com/

Chapter 8

Bugs 'n' Things

To me the outdoors is what you must pass through
in order to get from your apartment to the taxicab.

——Fran Lebowitz (1951-)

As a city kid growing up in Oakland, I spent a lot of time exploring the creek near my home for its wildness. But experiencing nature in the raw really came from the summers I spent living on my grandmother's farm at Irvington and the times of hiking and exploring in the High Sierras as a Boy Scout. When we had enough gas in our tank in the 1930s, we would all hop into my dad's 1929 four-door Essex sedan for a drive to the country. It was twenty-seven miles from Oakland to my mother's childhood home in Irvington, in southern Alameda County, a rich agricultural land located near Mission San Jose.

If the car didn't break down, the trip took less than an hour. Once we got going our top speed would reach forty-five miles per hour but small towns forced us to slow down along the way. The Oakland-San Jose state highway was two-lane and entirely blacktop. Most roads in the early 1930s had no painted centerline, separating the lanes. When the State of California finally did put them on most of its major roads, their guidance helped prevent a lot of accidents and pleased my father, who said more than once, "Somebody ought to give a medal to the guy who got the idea for those white lines."

For city kids, it was wonderful. We'd jump out excitedly to see these great open spaces and explore everything in sight. "They went wild out here," said my Uncle John, the farmer, who would show us how to milk a cow, hitch a horse to a wagon, and feed the pigs. After my grandfather O. C. Benbow died in 1929, bachelor John joined a couple of other relatives to help run Grandmother Annie Benbow's ten-acre farm. The house, which grandpa built himself, was a one-story, wood-framed structure with five-bedrooms. The acreage also included a barn, milk house, windmill, woodshed, feed house, chicken yard, and various other storage structures. My grandfather's principal cash crop came from his large orchard of prune trees, but he also had a few fig, peach, pear, walnut, and almond trees on the land to serve the family's own needs. Nearly everything we ate—meat, fruit and vegetables—was raised on the Benbow farm or those nearby.

From the time I was four years old, I can remember mornings when I awoke to sounds in the kitchen around five o'clock and ambling out there in my little bare feet to see my grandfather pulling on his boots, readying himself for milking the cows and feeding the animals—horses, pigs, turkeys, chickens, and domestic cats and dogs. My grandmother, too, would be preparing breakfast. She did all her cooking and baking on a big, cast-iron, wood-burning stove, which also heated the room. Later she would go outside to gather eggs from the chickens or vegetables from her small garden. In season we got walnuts, almonds, peaches, pears, apricots, and prunes. It was a self-sufficiency most people no longer have today.

With Pop at the wheel of our black Essex—the old car would have been a Graham Page in earlier days—and my mother beside him, we headed south on the two-lane blacktop Oakland-San Jose highway, all of us keeping our fingers crossed and hoping the car wouldn't break down along the way. When that happened, my brother and I would be bored sitting for what seemed hours by the side of the road, waiting.

Since there was no car radio to listen to in those days, my mother would encourage my six-year old brother Wallace and me to play fanciful games in the back seat.

"What color will the next passing car be?"

"Who can win the game of 'paper,' 'scissors,' or 'rock'?"

"Who remembers the best riddle?"

Whenever the car's motor sputtered and we came to a halt—which is what usually happened five miles south of the little town of

Hayward—my father would lift the side panels of the hood to diagnose the problem, poke around with a screw driver, and sometimes get us going by pouring a cup of gasoline into the carburetor.

Sometimes Pop found it necessary to ask whoever was in the front seat to get out of the car so that he could lift a small lid, set into the floor board or beneath the seat, to check whether a dead battery was the problem. Our breakdown could be a flat tire or an engine failure. At night it might be a headlight failure. These interruptions to our drive in the country seemed always to happen in the wide-open spaces, miles from gasoline stations, garages, or help of any kind. That's why old cars in those days had tool chests firmly attached to their running boards, containing the basic tools needed by the driver to repair the car himself when the time came. Otherwise you were stuck and hoped passersby would stop to help.

The hardest job was dealing with a flat tire, which meant pulling out the rubber inner tube, locating the leak, and patching it with a sticky adhesive, before hand-pumping it back up again. Of course, your first task was to get the wheel off the car and then pull the tire off the wheel. This meant lifting the car on a jack, then removing the tire and fixing it on the spot. If you were lucky, your vehicle carried a good spare tire, and you didn't need to fix the flat till you got home. The great idea of calling an auto club for help hadn't been invented yet. Or at least none existed as far as we knew and if it did, we couldn't afford the service anyway.

Cruising along the wide-open countryside was fun in those days. Every small town, village, or city we passed through had a special character of its own, starting with the lovely plaza in the center of San Leandro, next the city park in Hayward, then the corner store in Decoto, and finally the railway station in Niles. We'd slow down entering a town and then welcome the wide, open countryside when we could speed up at the other end. If my mother could find an extra nickel or dime in her purse, my father would park for a few minutes in Hayward so we could buy a five-cent ice cream cone, *Hershey* bar, or popcorn. *Crackerjacks* were great because each box had a surprise gift at the bottom.

Once we got going and returned to the road, the wind would whistle through the car windows as we enjoyed the smells and sights of the open land. After my Grandfather Benbow died in 1929, Grandma Annie needed help. So Helena Benbow and her husband Everett Hammond came down from Auburn to live and help with orchards, cows, horses, pigs, and chickens. This brought my cousins Wesley and Nelda to Irvington, who became neighbors of my other cousins, Ebba Rae and Lester Benbow, who lived on an adjacent farm south of my grandmother's place. Our lives were far less complicated in those days. Children of all ages were safe wandering anywhere they wanted to go. And having four cousins provided my brother Wallace and me with an *Our Gang* club of our own.

Indoors I turned my attention to looking around the nooks and crannies of my grandmother's large farmhouse, which had a particularly interesting basement. It was a one-story structure built by my grandfather before 1900, originally located on property he rented about a mile south of town but moved even closer a few years later. With help from neighbors and hired hands, the dwelling was jacked up, put on rollers, and towed by a team of horses, to the intersection of Cooks Road and the Oakland-San Jose highway. Wood-framed and spacious, it had five bedrooms, which easily accommodated both the parents and their eight children. It had indoor water for washing and cooking but no indoor toilets. Water came out of a deep well, pumped up by a windmill power to a huge tank on top of the building. Gravity brought it down into the house whenever you opened a tap.

Sometimes in a dry season, when there wasn't much wind, we were cautioned to be careful not to waste water because the tank level would be getting low. You washed your face and hands in cold water. Whenever you needed hot water for a bath, you had to heat it on the wood-burning kitchen stove. If you needed a privy, there was none in the house. Your daytime needs had to be satisfied by hurrying down the steps into the yard and using the outhouse next to the woodshed. The term used by locals for a two-hole facility was "Chic Sale." Old newspapers or an outdated Sears catalog were our equivalent of today's toilet rolls. Nobody used the outdoor facility at night when it was pitch black. At night older folks used the large pots kept under their beds for emergencies.

Tiring of the novelty of using an outhouse as a toilet, I began exploring other places around the farm to see what was different.

Nobody seemed to mind that a small boy was opening and examining everything he could find in old boxes and trunks stored in the basement, tucked away in closets, or gathering dust in the loft of the barn. Often my hunting expeditions led me to some wonderful discoveries, which I'd show to my Grandma Annie. Fortunately for me she would usually say, "You can have them, Gordon, if you want them." Thus I began assembling my own personal library of old books.

I hauled home dozens of textbooks on rhetoric, civics, and literature that had been used 30 or 40 years earlier by my mother, aunts, and uncles when they were school children. They attended Irvington Grammar School in the 1890s and early 1900s. Since no public library was located near me in Oakland, I welcomed everything I found at the farm as pirate's gold. My collection included biographies of great men, speeches by famous orators, and poetry and plays by Shakespeare, Henry Wadswsorth Longfellow, and Walt Whitman. I eagerly devoured all these and more.

There was wonderful fiction for aspiring poor boys like me. My favorite books were written by Horatio Alger, Jr. who told how poor boys could succeed in life by being trustworthy, helpful, friendly, and courteous—all the rules outlined in my Boy Scout handbook. This was what the Horatio Alger, Jr. stories taught, whether you found it in *Rough and Ready, Trust and True,* or his other titles. You also could find compelling adventure stories in the works of G. A. Henty, who introduced me to Hannibal in *The Young Carthaginians.* Stories about young men like Thomas Edison rising from humble beginnings to become inventors and scientists also influenced those of us looking for role models, especially my brother Wallace, who became a mechanical engineer.

Exploring everything by myself without teacher guidance, I finally stumbled upon a book, which captured my interest but stunted my growth as far as progress in education was concerned. Among these worn and tattered tomes which nobody had used for years, was a copy of a book called *The Real Diary of a Real Boy.* This one really caught my fancy because it was about the true experiences of someone my own age. I read this boy's first person account eagerly from cover to cover. It was written when the author Henry A. Shute was a Midwestern farm boy toward the end of the nineteenth century. Although Shute's memoir inspired me to start my own diary, it also led me to imitate his style, which unfortunately was ungrammatical, full of misspelled words, and definitely not what my teachers expected me to know about good English. Years later I saw the error of my ways. That experience taught me to be choosy about whom you imitate.

Then one day something happened that seemed unbelievable. I'd just come home from ice-skating with friends at a rink in downtown Oakland and entered the door, when my mother approached, and with a smile, handed me a letter. She said, "It came this morning, Gordon, and it's from back east." Curious as to what was inside, especially since the envelope carried an important-looking return address, I ripped it open. Inside I found a letter from a newspaper syndicate, which said, "Congratulations. Your drawing has been selected for publication in our Sunday sections."

I had won a contest and newspapers were going to publish my cartoon in Sunday papers from coast to coast. How did this happen? Well, I'd made an original sketch, showing how the shape of the state of Illinois could be turned into the likeness of a dapper gentleman with a derby hat. Winning the contest earned me no cash or other tangible reward, but it did being me recognition, because my drawing was going to be published along with my name and address.

What followed was completely unexpected—fan mail. On publication of my cartoon, letters began arriving in the mailbox addressed to the artist. They came from readers scattered about the United States, three of whom got my attention—one from Idaho, a second from Virginia, and a third from New York. All three were girls and each wanted me as a pen pal and invited me to correspond with them, which I promptly did.

Totally unaware of the birds and the bees in 1935—when my drawing first appeared—I was happy at the time to hear from anyone, even a strange young man writing from New Jersey, who left me somewhat puzzled by what he wrote in his fan letter, which went something like this: "I love you. I am eager to see you and am coming out to California as soon as possible. I'm sure you'll like me and that we'll be happy living together, etc."

While it did seem a bit strange to me, as I wondered how anyone could truly like me who didn't know me, I soon discovered what he wrote truly alarmed both of my parents. So Pop sat down immediately, took pen in hand, composed a strongly worded message, and air mailed it to the young man with a firm warning: "Stay away from my son. Do not come here. If you attempt to contact my boy, I guarantee you that the police will arrest you and put you in jail." That ended that.

Of the three girls who had sent me fan letters, two got married, and only one kept up the correspondence. She was Lillian Wagers of Yonkers, New York, a young woman four years older, who arranged to meet me at a soda fountain near Radio City Music Hall on a trip east I took several years later. When I finally showed up—a gangly, immature, teenager, hardly dry behind the ears—I apparently was not what she had expected. There was no indication anything was wrong when we met for our first date near Times Square, enjoyed ice cream at a soda fountain, saw a science fiction movie at Radio City Music Hall, and arranged to meet where I was staying the next day. The only trouble was that she never showed up.

I was left cooling my heels at the YMCA all day long, waiting for her to appear, and finally got the idea she didn't want to see me any longer. Since our correspondence stopped and she left no note at the "Y," I wondered for years afterward what was wrong with me until I finally figured out she was expecting an older man.

My understanding of the opposite sex, or sheer lack of it, seemed to have begun that day. Being seen in Sunday newspapers nationwide and getting fan mail from all over the country was pretty heady stuff for a growing boy and maybe a bit too much to handle yourself when you're only a teenage boy. There were lessons here that I was slow in learning.

While the country boy understood a lot about "bugs 'n' things," the city kid still had a lot to learn about "the birds and the bees"!

GOOGLE GUIDE

Chapter 8: Bugs 'n' Things

For more on this subject, try these:

"My First Summer in the Sierra," by John Muir. (book).
Find title at Google Books: http://books.google.com/

"Roosevelt Addresses Boy Scouts (1935)." (newsreel).
http://www.archive.org/details/1935-02-11_Roosevelt_Addresses_
Boy_Scouts/

"Bugs 'n' Things," by Gordon Greb. (column).
http://bugthings.blogspot.com/

For a longer listing, go to the book's web site:

Google Brain Book: http://googlebrainbook.blogspot.com/

Chapter 9

A Gentleman of the Press

*As a reporter, I like to keep in the middle
and be disliked by both sides.*

——Jimmy Breslin (1930-)

We left Oakland in 1937, when my dad got steady employment with the Southern Pacific Company, took a veterans' loan, and moved us into a new home in San Leandro (population: 14,500). Three years later when Editor George Thompson of the *San Leandro News* thought of hiring me as a cub reporter right out of high school, I can still remember him rubbing his chin and saying with some hesitancy, "Gosh, you'll be on the police beat and you look so darn young, hardly dry behind the years. I wish you looked older." That's when I made a wish that came true.

San Leandro began celebrating the opening of the Golden Gate International Exposition on Treasure Island with "Western Days" in the spring of 1939. That's when I had an appointment to see the editor seated at his desk, wearing overalls and a checkered shirt instead of a suit and tie. He had happily joined the celebrity mood, sporting a large red bandana around his neck, a huge black cowboy hat pushed back from his head, and a face darkened by a slow growth of beard.

As he looked me over through wire-rimmed glasses, Mr. Thompson seemed to be quite elderly in his ruffled clothing, plump body, and receding hairline, but in truth, he was still a vigorous gentleman in his thirties. But no matter how he looked, I tried to keep my nervousness under control, realizing this was the man who held my future in his grasp. If I got on the payroll of his paper, it would be my first full-time job as a reporter and for that I would do almost anything. It was called the *San Leandro News* at that time, but later became the *News-Observer.*

That morning, preparing to see the editor, I once again tried shaving with my father's razor blade in the vain hope of growing first-time whiskers. As part of the activities promoting the opening of the San Francisco World's Fair, the honorary sheriff of the city's Chamber of Commerce was on duty at the city plaza, ready to throw clean-shaven men into its makeshift hoosegow for not obeying the rules. The judge of the kangaroo court would look kindly on any local citizen dressed in western garb but being beardless was courting trouble.

When I donned my own cowboy outfit that morning, I was trying to look as sharp as possible for the job interview. Only a seventeen-year old dressed up to look like westerner Gary Cooper, who had no beard or wrinkles on his face, could possibly have hoped to impress an interrogator this way. But with youth being against me, I was willing to try anything. Every kid leaving high school like myself had to confront the same question, "Have you done anything like this before? Tell me, young man, what's your experience?"

When Thompson asked to see my work, all I could hand him was kid stuff: clippings of news stories I'd published in the two school papers I'd edited, *The Flash* at Frick Junior High and *The Cargo* at San Leandro High School, together with samples of what I'd done for the children's pages of the *Oakland Post Enquirer* and *Oakland Tribune.* My best stuff, which had appeared in the *Post Enquirer*, earned me crisp, new one dollar bills each time the paper ran one of my stories or cartoons. By today's standards, that might be regarded as small change. But it was big money for a teen-ager during the last days of the Great Depression.

When I showed up at the old one-story *San Leandro News* building at 955 East 14th Street, the paper's assistant editor Dick Loomis caught me coming into the office, called me over, and confronted me with grave doubts about one of the stories I'd included in my "string" (meaning my clippings). As I stood patiently waiting, he accused me of copying someone else's work and claimed it couldn't possibly be mine.

"Come clean, kid," he said. "You took that 'Bugs 'n Things' column from somebody else, didn't you? No little kid like you wrote anything like that!"

Although Loomis was destined to become a Pulitzer Prize contender as an investigative reporter, he was off his mark on that one. I calmly explained that every piece I'd submitted was my own work, whether he wanted to believe it or not. Although I didn't need to tell him, I was going into the interview knowing Editor Thompson had seen some examples of my work years earlier and on that count I had nothing to fear. The piece in question had appeared in the *Scout Scribe*, a publication of the Oakland Area Council of the Boy Scouts of America for several thousand scouts and their leaders living in Alameda County.

Eager to be a young reporter, I had joined the *Scout Scribe* staff at the age of fifteen in 1936, was assigned the outdoor beat by the editor, and began writing "Bugs 'n' Things" for every issue. It was lucky for me that Editor Thompson saw one of my teen-age pieces when it came out and had been impressed enough to send me a note, saying, "Drop in sometime and talk over your writing interests." Now here I was three years later about to meet Thompson again and get the chance I'd been waiting for. But was I good enough to be a real reporter?

When I'd chosen newspaper work as my career in the seventh grade, the school authorities immediately put me on the vocational skills track. I began taking classes in wood shop, metal shop, and print shop instead of literature, higher mathematics, and the sciences. My parents asked why I had been kept out of the college preparatory program and were told by a school counselor, "If your son wants to become a newspaperman, a college degree isn't necessary." Someone at the school had phoned the city desk of the *Oakland Tribune* and was told college degrees weren't needed to become a reporter.

My mother had higher ambitions for me. Being someone who loved English, literature, and the arts, she regretted not finishing San Jose Teachers College due to poor health when she was young. She knew what I would be missing. She also knew I'd benefit by going to Bay Area universities like Cal or Stanford. So she insisted that despite my erratic grade record, I was intelligent enough to handle the college work and should be reassigned to college preparatory classes.

None of this was known to me at the time. I liked things the way they were. But one day, much to my surprise, I was taken from class by an administrator, driven to Mills College, and told to be seated at a desk facing a middle-aged woman thumbing through some papers. The only other person in the room was a much younger woman watching all this and taking notes off to one side. The grey-haired lady across from me looked agreeable enough and put me at ease.

"Gordon," I heard her say. "Your parents know you're here. We're going to ask you a series of questions and give you a few problems to solve to find out what you like and what you're good at. The questions and problems I'm going to pose won't be too unusual, but in each case it's important for you to consider carefully and give each of them your best answer!"

Everything about this situation told me it was important. I felt that by being singled out, given special attention, and taken away from school, this was a good reason to do my best on everything that was about to happen. After about an hour had passed I was finished and was taken back to school where everything returned to normal. Maybe my parents were told the results but I never found out. All I know is that the following term in the ninth grade I began the college preparatory program.

When it came to qualifying for the job at the *San Leandro News,* all I could offer the editor were "As" in two years of high school journalism classes. Other than that all I had done was some work on apparently small and insignificant publications—the *Whittier School Snap, Troop 52 Bugle, Katz Meow, Frick Flash, Slate Scribblings, Open Road for Boys, Scout Scribe,* and *San Leandro Cargo.* At the age of eight I had posted announcements on a bulletin board for neighbors to stop and read while walking past our house. Later I buried "time capsules" in our backyard at the age of ten (actually notes in sealed cans or bottles) asking questions like, "Will there be another war?" or "When will the depression be over?"

No matter how unimportant they seemed, I knew my experience had so far taught me the fundamentals of printing from Guttenberg to the present day. By reason of those activities I had learned how to print cartoons from a linoleum block; pump the handle on an old fashioned colonial press; use a stylus to cut a stencil for mimeograph machine;

and turn copy from a typewriter into galleys of linotype and lock them into forms for publication on a flatbed press.

None of this is what we talked about that morning because I remember that Thompson didn't have a minute to waste. After regretting how young I looked, he got up from the desk, shook my hand, and said, "You've got the job, Gordon." Then he added, "I'm starting you off this summer at eight dollars a week. When Stackhouse comes in, I'll have him show you the ropes."

That's how Glenn Stackhouse, a confident young reporter of medium height, came into my life. We worked together for the next three summers covering fires, accidents, thefts, council meetings, court hearings, and meetings of the Rotary, Lions, and Chamber of Commerce. Here was a man who obviously loved his work, taught me the tricks of the trade of gathering and reporting the news, and worked hard at it.

From the first morning we met, he took me over to City Hall to get acquainted with the police department and city manager's office, where he carefully gave me tips on how to do my job. Since that day, I've always been grateful to this man for breaking me in. On my last conversation with him in San Francisco, I felt proud to be talking to a first class newspaperman, remembering what he said sharply to me one day when I thanked him helping me to become a journalist.

"We're not journalists," he said. "We're newspapermen! And that's what you're going to be when we're done with you!"

Right to the end, that's what he was. He was assistant bureau manager for United Press news service in San Francisco when he died of a heart attack twenty years later. I found this out from a newspaper, the *San Francisco Chronicle*, and remembered that obits were the first thing he had taught me to write as a cub reporter on the *San Leandro News*.

By that time I had become a full-fledged newspaperman myself, realizing it when nobody questioned my press pass when I showed it at the gates to the Golden Gate International Exposition on Treasure Island. That was easy to understand. A few dozen hairs were beginning to show on my unshaven face, and my beard was beginning to grow!

GOOGLE GUIDE

Chapter 9: A Gentleman of the Press

For more on this subject, try these:

"The Front Page - Original Trailer 1974." (movie trailer).
Find title at YouTube: http://www.youtube/

"Newspaper Story (1950) (encyclopedia film). Time: 16:29 min.
http://www.archive.org/details/NewspaperSto/

"The Golden Gate International Exposition (1939)." (home movie).
http://www.archive.org/details/Californ1939/

For a longer listing, go to the book's web site:

Google Brain Book: http://googlebrainbook.blogspot.com/

Chapter 10

The America I Saw in 1941

America is a large, friendly dog in a very small room.
Every time it wags its tail, it knocks over a chair.

——Arnold Toynbee (1889-1975)

It was a fine day when I boarded the Southern Pacific passenger train in San Jose on May 26, 1941, headed for Los Angeles, which was the beginning of a 30-day journey around the United States in what was then called the Grand Circle Tour.

I can remember looking out the window at the passing California landscape en route to the south, wondering what lay ahead, and felt inwardly excited by the prospect of seeing people and places I wanted to know more about, which oddly enough lay at the stops ahead of me in my own country.

As a nineteen-year old reporter for the *San Leandro News,* curious about everything and blessed with a big nose for news, I was already looking around for stories to write about and felt I could handle anything; that is, except for what really happened. I needed to carefully spend every nickel and dime for this trip, all the savings I'd earned working summers for the *San Leandro News.* But what really helped me the most was being a teen-age son of a locomotive engineer that entitled me to ride trains free of charge anywhere in the USA by simply showing my special pass.

If my editor back home had said at the start of this trip, "Gordon, what do you plan to ask President Roosevelt when you get to his press conference?" I'd have said, "Hold on, George! What makes you think the White House press secretary is going to let me in?" But strange as it may seem, as things turned out, I indeed got the proper credentials from United Press to let guards examine me at the west entrance and finally grant me admittance.

While accomplishments of this kind may have seemed to have been the highlight of the trip, I now realize that certain things much more important were happening to me at the time and that they constituted its real value. As I crossed the country, seeing cities and towns, historic sites, military bases, and people of all kinds, shapes, and colors for the first time, I was slowly losing my innocence.

On that day of my departure I considered myself an isolationist, convinced I would be doing the right thing to tell President Roosevelt to keep us out of war, not wishing to repeat, as did many Americans, the awful suffering and carnage of the First World War. But before the year was out, I became convinced war was inevitable and that we all had to pull together to win it. But what I hadn't yet comprehended were subtle changes occurring both to my country and to me even before bombs fell on Pearl Harbor six months later.

As I study my old 1941 trip diary today, I see that it reveals the most extraordinary truths from the most ordinary of things. What I find from today's perspective is that the record of this trip now seems as revealing as a strange artifact dug up by Egyptologists or the insights into seventieth century England from the diary of Samuel Pepys.

According to my diary, here's how America has changed since my trip in 1941:

1. **Great network radio programs are gone.** It was really fun to get free entertainment over the radio in the 1940s but we lost a national treasure when those wonderful "live" comedy, drama, and variety shows were taken off the airwaves. In the 1930s and 40s, audiences loved all the coast-to-coast shows being produced from the NBC and CBS studios in Hollywood, Chicago, and New York.

Radio attracted huge national audiences for shows like the *Jack Benny Program, Bing Crosby Show, Mr. District Attorney, Lux Radio Theatre, One Man's Family, First Nighter, It Pays to Be Ignorant, Your Hit Parade,* and many more. I happily laughed and applauded when lucky enough to see these movie stars in person on my visit to the NBC and

CBS studios in Hollywood in 1941—Edward G. Robinson, Claudette Colbert, Shirley Temple, and John Barrymore. It was easy for studio audiences to get free tickets to their shows in the old days.

You can have much the same experience today by going to London. There the BBC still presents radio shows before live audiences. Or you could check the listings to find out when Garrison Keillor would be bringing his *Prairie Home Companion* to your own hometown for public radio.

2. **Great Hollywood movie studios are gone!** Of the eight major movie giants, none are entirely their former selves today. When I visited Hollywood in 1941 I saw Gene Tierney and Randolph Scott doing a scene on the sound stage of 20th Century Fox. According to my diary, I must have been standing in Gene Tierney's way, for someone put her hand on my shoulder and politely asked to squeeze past me.

In order to see 20th Century Fox's vast outdoor sets, a tour guide took me around by car to view all the make-believe streets and villages of Buenos Aires, London, Bangkok, Bombay, London, and New York on the back lot. The studio had created these facades for such films as *Down Argentine Way, Cavalcade, How Green Was My Valley, The Grapes of Wrath, The King and I,* and *Hello, Dolly.*

Years later I when I returned to the same spot, I found nothing remained of those old sets but in their place was a massive, high-rise hotel where I was staying for an Associated Press conference. The back lot had become a new business development called the Century City complex and if you looked around elsewhere in tinsel town, you'd find that other studios like Disney and Universal Studios had grown into amusement parks.

3. **America's great passenger train service is gone**. You could go nearly anywhere by rail when I planned my trip around the country in 1941. When the *Sunset Limited* arrived at El Paso, Texas, from Los Angeles, I got off that morning, took a tour bus to the Carlsbad Caverns, and returned in time to catch another train going east that same evening. Such quick connections are no longer possible today.

I slept soundly in a coach seat on most nights and could get three meals a day (breakfast, lunch and dinner) for an average cost of about $1.30 a day. At various stations, Travelers' Aid supplied me with free maps, schedules, and directions to good restaurants, and the YMCA provided cheap lodging, averaging sixty-five cents a night.

With such frugality I made the entire thirty-day journey on less than seventy dollars. If that seems ridiculously low, it represented every penny I earned working all summer long on the newspaper. Unfortunately today's Amtrak does not come close to replicating what we've lost. So I'm afraid we'll need to wait till people get tired of high gas prices, crowded airports, and jam-packed highways before we'll ever again enjoy the wonderful railway service we once had. However, you can still find great rail travel today in Europe or Japan.

4. **Racial segregation is gone from the South.** When the train entered Texas in 1941, it took me into a different world because I had my first sighting of drinking fountains marked "white" and "colored" at Houston. Next I found out the entire train was segregated, blacks in one car, whites in the others, as we moved toward New Orleans.

I had become acquainted with my seat companion, a Chinese wool merchant named Mr. Minshan Hu, who expressed surprise by what was going on, saying, "I heard so much about your democracy where everyone is supposed to be free and equal, and yet here I find people divided." All I could do was agree with him.

Not until an American Negro soldier spoke to me in my hospital ward, back from overseas during World War II, did I get a hint of the coming civil rights movement. He came over to talk to me at my bedside and finally said, "We're not going to take it any more. This is my country, I fought for it, and I want my rights." So I knew change was coming. And when it finally happened, it swept barriers away all the way up to and including who could occupy the White House.

5. **New York will always be New York.** When I first saw them in 1941, they were an astonishing sight—a line of 24 long-legged girls known as the Roxyettes—a high-kicking dance team at the Roxy Theater at 153 West 50th Street between 6th and 7th avenues. These precision dancers were moved a few years later to the Radio City Music Hall, where the troupe's name was changed to the Rockettes. Now they're as much an institution as New York City's Statue of Liberty and Grand Central Station.

Although my wanderings also took me to Rockefeller Center, Times Square, the Museum of Modern Art, and the Automat, I think the Algonquin Hotel still holds the most memories for me because I went there looking to see famous writers like Robert Benchley, Dorothy Parker, and Harold Ross of magazine fame. But alas, they were gone. So next time you're in New York, I recommend your getting tickets to see the fabulous Rockettes. No need to worry because they'll still be there.

6. **The Loyal Opposition in politics is an endangered species**. At New Haven, Connecticut, I heard a remarkable Republican deliver a commencement address at Yale University in 1941. Wendell Willkie had been defeated for the presidency by Franklin D. Roosevelt the previous year, but he refused to let party politics dissuade him from approving Roosevelt's policy of helping Britain in its desperate fight against Nazi Germany.

When war finally came, Roosevelt sent Willkie as his special envoy to Britain, Russia, and China, which led him to write *One World*, a book proposing a special international body to keep world peace. As hard as I've looked around, I can't find a Republican like him on the scene anywhere today.

7. **Chicago will never give up**. Wrigley Field is one of baseball's oldest ballparks, where fans come out to see the Cubs play whether they are winning or losing. That's where I saw my first major league baseball game in 1941, sitting among stalwart fans who kept coming to see the Cubs play despite their blowing World Series or Pennant chances by stupid errors, bad luck, or someone casting a spell. Despite having one of the oldest stadiums, originally built in 1916, the Cubs seem to be perfectly happy still playing there, which seems to prove that winning isn't everything.

8. **Presidents don't always know the truth or tell it if they do.** I got up early on my last day in Washington, D.C. on June 13, hurrying to shave, shower, and put on my best suit and tie, not wanting to be late for my appointment to see President Franklin D. Roosevelt. All arrangements to admit me had been made by United Press with press secretary Stephen Early, and I certainly wanted to look my best when I arrived.

So when the guardhouse officer let me through the west gate to the White House by locating my name on the approved list, he pointed me to the proper entrance and I bounded up the paved pathway, admiring the grass and flowers, and thinking about what was coming, I wondered, "What question should I ask the President?" After making my way into the annex and checking in at the front desk, my hopes were dashed a few minutes later when an assistant press secretary came out, introduced himself, and gave me the bad news:

"I'm sorry to tell you this, Mr. Greb, but the President has a bad cold his morning and has cancelled his press conference. I'm sure we can arrange for you to see him next week if you'll return."

I could not return. It would extend my trip another week, which I couldn't afford on my limited budget. Furthermore I'd already made plans to catch a train out of Washington's Union Station that afternoon for appointments in New York City. So I retraced my steps back to the hotel, packed my bags, and departed Washington, D.C. without ever meeting the President.

Today I believe there was a "big story" right under our collective reporters' noses but it was impossible for any of us to realize it at the time. It's my firm belief the president expected war would break out with the Axis powers in mid-June 1941 by reason of certain strict measures he was taking against them at that time.

I believe Roosevelt did not have a cold. That was an excuse to hide something else. The President believed he was forcing Germany, Italy, and Japan to declare war on the United States at any moment. Here are the provocative measures which he thought could have led us into war sooner than it did:

May 21—The President in a radio address warned the nation that we were in imminent danger and declared we were in "an unlimited state of national emergency."

May 27—Roosevelt next announced the United States was aiding and assisting all nations resisting Nazi aggression.

June 13— He cancelled his regular press conference because of "a cold."

June 14—Roosevelt suddenly announced he was "freezing" all assets of Germany and Italy in the United States and approved the seizure of their vessels in American ports and closing down of their consulates.

June 15—Carrying out orders from the White House, port authorities blocked the loading of oil onto a Japanese tanker at Philadelphia on the grounds America needed the oil for itself.

June 21—War finally broke out! But not against us! Instead Hitler had launched a secret plan of his own—a surprise attack on the U.S.S.R.—that sent a huge military thrust into Russian territory, extending from the Arctic to the Black Sea. Hitler sought a quick victory in the east and could not afford to expose his back to us. It would have been foolish for him to open up a second front against the United States while fully engaged with a major foe in the east.

The amazing conclusion for me is that we could have been involved in World War II in June 1941 instead of December 1941. But Roosevelt, not knowing of Hitler's secret war plans, was as surprised as I was on learning where and when it actually happened. By the time I learned that Germany had attacked Russia, I was listening to the radio in a lounge car heading west out of Chicago, en route home by way of Seattle, Washington, and Portland, Oregon. I arrived home by train on June 24, unpacked my bags, and began covering auto accidents, city council meetings, and club meetings the following week for the *San Leandro News*. When you're a reporter, that's what you do!

GOOGLE GUIDE

Chapter 10: The America I Saw in 1941

For more on this subject, try these:

"Duke Ellington: 'Take the "A" Train.'" (song).
Find title at YouTube: http://www.youtube.com/

"His Girl Friday (1940)." (Columbia feature length film) Time: 92 min. http://www.archive.org/details/his girl_friday/

"Robert Benchley and the Knights of the Algonquin" (film). Time: 2:04 min. Find title at YouTube: http://www.youtube.com/

For a longer listing, go to the book's web site:

Google Brain Book: http://googlebrainbook.blogspot.com/

Chapter 11

A Prisoner in a Chinese Cookie Factory

If you think education is expensive—try ignorance.

——Derek Bok (1930-)

The man who best understood the feelings of children was the stand-up comedian Rodney Dangerfield. By admitting, "I don't get no respect," this man (who happened to be my own age) was able to build a highly successful career. He talked about having the same put-downs and humiliations growing up as a kid as I had.

Almost from my first day in kindergarten I was like that tiny character in Charles Shultz' comic strip Peanuts, carrying a blanket around wherever he went, because he needed love and security. Teachers can, if they're really good, build self-confidence in children. Or lacking empathy, they can take it away.

Those few who made my life miserable made the mistake of dismissing me as a first-class "won't-pay-attention" dumbbell or a smart aleck kid who had a tendency to talk too much. However, lucky for me, there were others who, by reason of their own good judgments, disagreed with those put-downers and came to my rescue. Thanks to their support, along with that from my parents, I was ultimately able to face obstacles put in my way and was left with the hope of achieving something someday.

Most of my Oakland public school teachers of the l920s and 30s did their best. The one I can remember particularly well was Mrs. Finger of Fremont High School, who tried to shake us out of our lethargy and get everyone ready for the tenth grade. More than that, she was actually trying her best to prepare us for life. At our end-term orientation she had this final advice for us wide-eyed innocents when she said, "As you're getting older every day, time is precious. Soon you'll be young adults. That's why you should buckle down right now, prepare yourself for the future, and use this time wisely so you won't be sorry later."

Shortly before I graduated from high school, my science teacher Mr. Qualmaltz got into a discussion about me among colleagues in the faculty lunchroom, saying flatly I wasn't college material. "Take it from me," he told fellow teachers. "He will never survive the rigorous academic demands of the University of California. I gave him an 'F' in physics class because he just couldn't cut it."

I found this out from my journalism teacher, Mr. James MacDonald, who took me into his confidence, saying he felt certain I'd prove the science teacher wrong when I went to college. My other strong supporter was Mr. Raymond Riese, my social science teacher, who had encouraged me to enter several public speaking contests, one of which I'd won. Both men knew me well because I'd taken their classes for two years straight.

What upset Mr. Qualmaltz was a state ballot proposition, which I had strongly favored in a school debate. If passed by the voters, the new law would pay the elderly "$30 Every Thursday" by requiring the State of California to print new currency. A similar idea had worked elsewhere. For example, South Dakota had operated its own state-owned bank since 1919, reducing taxes because all its earnings belonged to the state. But Mr. Qualmaltz feared such a proposal would endanger teachers' pay.

Since the question for many of us leaving high school was, "Why Go to College?" I had argued in favor of higher education in a speech I delivered in an oratorical competition in my junior year. But the judges chose someone else as the winner. At the urging of my teachers, I tried again in the spring term of 1939, arguing against our getting involved in another European war with the topic, "What Price Glory?" The result was that I tied for First Place—which I shared with my Japanese-American classmate Lily Kawahara—who also was opposed to our going to war. Isolationism was being debated nationally and the local weekly newspaper printed both of our speeches in their entirety.

When the time came for me to enroll at the University of California, it became necessary for me to get a job to cover my college expenses. I needed money for tuition, supplies, books, meals, and the daily commute between Berkeley and my home, riding on buses and streetcars. The idea of joining a fraternity or taking a room near campus was financially out of the question.

During each fall and spring semesters, I earned $5.75 per week (twenty-five-cents per hour), pumping gas at a Texaco station; and took home eight dollars per week working three months of each summer vacation as a full-time reporter for the *San Leandro News-Observer*. Needless to say I had to pinch pennies and stick to a very strict budget.

In my junior year in college I had a lucky break. I came up with an idea for a weekly fifteen-minute radio news program with my friend Dave Houser, sports writer for the San Leandro newspaper. But before we could start this newscast on KROW, we first had to sell the idea to the publisher Al Neish. On the day of our appointment to see him, we carried a portable phonograph machine into his office, plugged it into a wall socket, and asked him to hear a recording of the proposed newscast.

As soon as Neish heard the trumpets of the opening theme, identifying his newspaper as the sponsor, the publisher leaped up from his desk, opened the door, and shouted to everyone in the outer editorial offices, "Get in here and hear this. We're on the radio!" Thus began something entirely new for the San Francisco Bay Area. With the inauguration of our newscast, "Observing the News," in 1942, it became the first all-local news program for listeners in the north state. We did it at 8 o'clock every Friday morning over KROW until both of us joined the army a year later.

Berkeley at the time claimed to be the largest university in the country. When I walked through the university's Sather Gate onto the campus that first day, registering with Cal's twenty-four thousand students, I easily understood why it had the reputation of being the greatest. I found myself mingling shoulder to shoulder among the most talented and ambitious people I'd ever seen in my life. Being among these outwardly confident and self-assured students told me I was in for some stiff competition.

On its vast campus, spread out over 178 acres, I needed a map to find my way around the campus and get to where my classes were to take place. What impressed me the most was its beautiful academic environment, situated on a sloping Berkeley hillside, among grass and trees, with lovely views to the west of San Francisco Bay and the Golden Gate.

When I first encountered Cal's famous faculty standing at their podiums, they seemed like gods. Seated among hundreds in large lecture halls, I was awed by such men as Cheney of paleontology, Erickson of political science, Hynes of geology, Smyth of history, and Tolman of psychology. Topping the list of great orators was UC president Robert Gordon Sproul, who got students out of their seats, standing and cheering, whenever he spoke to assemblies in the Men's Gym.

As for Berkeley's distinguished professors, they regarded themselves the equal of Harvard's, justifiably proud of their own Nobel Prizes, academic status worldwide, and generous research grants. Their stature seemed to be represented in the buildings themselves, particularly the imposing Campanile, Wheeler Hall, and the Library.

In the light of all this eminence, what made me feel like a prisoner in a Chinese Cookie Factory soon after I arrived? To answer that question, I need to confess my shortcomings and explain how these setbacks nearly bounced me out of Cal during my freshman year. They were:

(1) Failing to pass the English "A" exam given all entering students.

(2) Getting a below-average grade in a required five-unit Spanish course.

(3) Receiving a 4-F classification in the ROTC program.

When you suddenly awaken up to the fact you may be tossed out of the university, it boggles the mind. Is it any wonder I began asking myself, "Could Mr. Qualmaltz have been right?" Unless I straightened things out within the year, I'd be out on my ear. For me the possibility of flunking out of the University of California before I had a chance to get started left me feeling, as my dad would say, "as dumb as a doornail" and "up a creek without a paddle."

In addition to these academic challenges, I also found myself entangled in a spider's web of class traditions. Starting Cal was somewhat like being a stranger in a strange land, baffled by its mysterious languages and customs. One example of my troubled college life came to me shortly after my arrival. Stopping me on the campus one day was an upper classman, who easily identified me as a freshman.

"Why aren't you wearing your beanie?" he demanded to know. "If I catch you next time without one, you'll be sorry."

What he called a "beanie" was a small Blue and Gold cap I'd seen for sale in the Associated Students Bookstore. Negligent "frosh" were warned they would be paddled by sophomores if caught without one. Despite the danger, I don't remember ever being fearful enough of sophomores to wear one regularly. Nor did I ever worry about being paddled. But I did buy a beanie at the Associated Students Bookstore as a souvenir, which explains why that cap still sits proudly on my hat rack at home today, as good as new.

Then dark clouds started gathering over my happy-go-lucky life. My first bad news was being notified that I had flunked the English "A" Exam, which was required of everyone entering the university. For someone who had been editor-in-chief of his high school newspaper, this was a terrible shock. But worse than deflating my ego was the damage it did to my pocket book.

If you failed the English test, you were required to take a remedial course (so called Bonehead English) for which the university collected, as best I remember it, an extra twenty-five dollars for its trouble. Since I'd already paid about twenty-seven dollars for tuition and was earning only $5.75 each week at my Texaco Gasoline station job, this new assessment blew a big hole in my budget.

Fortunately the remedial English instructor, who welcomed us to class the first day, told us how to escape from this Chinese Cookie Factory. "If you get an 'A' on the first midterm," he announced to all us boneheads, "you'll be excused from the course and also be refunded the money you paid to get here."

That startling news had me immediately sitting up straight and alert to everything the teacher said in that classroom from that day forward. No freshman mastered an English Grammar book quicker or more thoroughly than I after hearing this. By the time of the first major test, I had Nouns chasing Active Verbs, Phrases fighting madly to get into Complex Sentences and Subjects happily walking down the aisle to marry Predicates.

Yes, I definitely got an "A" on that first midterm, was excused from the class, and was handed a refund check for twenty-five dollars within a matter of days. While nobody actually apologized, I was pleased to know the university seemed to want to deal fairly with each and every student, a policy I've long remembered and deeply appreciated.

The next shock came when I learned that I had been put on probation for not achieving an acceptable GPA (grade point average). What precipitated this disaster was a less than passing grade from Miss Lamb, my Spanish language teacher, who gave me a "D" in a five-unit course. That took my university average below a "C" and threatened to "drop kick" me out of college.

There were just too many outside obligations taking up my time and interfering with my study habits. Yet solving that problem is what I had to do. I spent two hours commuting round-trip to the university and three hours pumping gas for Texaco every day. Since I couldn't move near campus and couldn't quit my job, this meant I had to use my commute hours more efficiently. So I used the time spent on buses and streetcars to study.

If I were to successfully accomplish some academic handsprings, I needed to figure out how to get As and Bs and began asking various friends how they did it. After asking older students I'd known in high school, this is what they told me:

(1) "Whenever you think you've been graded unfairly by a reader, see the professor and make your case for a reconsideration."

(2) "Get hold of Phi Beta Notes and commit them to memory. Since they're prepared by the best students at the university, their summations of the lectures are excellent preparation for exams because they cover everything you'll need to know."

(3) "Take a snap course. We can recommend several. Take any one of them and you'll get an A or B for sure."

Although the course I chose seemed a bit risky, I picked it out because it came highly recommended—Oriental Languages 10A— which could have ended up as a stupid choice since I'd already had a disastrous experience with Spanish. But I did it anyway out of sheer desperation. A short, plump Chinese gentleman welcomed us into his two-unit Oriental Languages course by making a surprise announcement. His lectures, he said, would deal primarily with Chinese culture and philosophy.

"You won't have any required reading," he said. "Select what you want for the text yourself; any book you think you'll enjoy; and one which hopefully will increase your knowledge and understanding."

A course with no defined structure? This was something I'd never experienced before and I wondered what he had in mind. Consequently I listened intently to everything this innovative professor had to say from that first day on and never missed one of his classes. This kindly professor talked about the philosophy of Yin and Yang, people and places in Chinese history, the geography of the land, and reasons for the conflict raging at that time on the Asian continent between the communists and General Chiang Kai-Shek.

Later he asked: "If you could choose between living a long and happy life but never thereafter to be remembered, or a person who would die young but be remembered as a great hero, which would you choose?" It left me undecided and puzzled, and kept troubling me for years afterward because I could never actually decide. However, now that I'm an octogenarian—an OAP (Old Age Pensioner) in England—and not a dead hero, I obviously know the answer. Fate decided it for me.

When the final examination was handed out, my Chinese professor gave us one question to answer: "What did you learn from your text?" The tome I had chosen for my text was an old nineteenth century schoolbook I'd picked up on my grandmother's farm. Since it was small enough to fit into my pocket, I took it along every day to read while riding the streetcar. In it was a wonderful collection of poems, essays, and works by great literary giants like Wordsworth, Tennyson, Longfellow, Emerson, and others.

Giving serious thought to my answer, I realized how remarkable it was that we, the living, were still able to reach the thoughts of the great minds of the past through their books, which had dawned on me while reading my chosen text. Extrapolating on that theme, I earned an "A" in Oriental Studies and got the key to unlock the door of the Chinese Cookie Factory. That grade, combined with good grades in others, reinstated me as a regular student, set me back on the path to a Bachelor of Arts degree, and reinvigorated my overall morale.

The last blow was the hardest to overcome. It was my rejection from the ROTC program for reasons of poor health. It didn't matter scholastically but it mattered a great deal after Pearl Harbor when I wanted to join the military. Nearly every male student at Cal was deciding whether to be a draftee or volunteer. Since the armed services were actively encouraging college men to join their officer training programs—the Navy, the Air Corps, and the Marines—I volunteered for each one, only to be turned down one after the other for poor eyesight.

With only one more recruiting office to visit, I wondered what the army would find wrong with me. But by a stroke of luck I was asked to sit in an outer room before visiting the medical doctor. Finding the door open to the eye clinic from where I sat, I could easily read every line on the huge "E" eye chart wearing my glasses. While waiting, I memorized every line on the chart and when examined, was able to recite everything correctly down to the smallest letters.

Then turning to me, the optomitrist said with a knowing smile, "Where are your eye glasses, son? You obviously wear glasses from the indentations around your nose." Then he assured me all was not lost. He told me the U.S. Army was taking everyone whose vision was properly corrected by glasses. So I put mine on and had little trouble passing the test, which got me in.

By this time all eligible men were being called up—students from Cal and colleges everywhere—who were needed to fight a ruthless and determined enemy. Millions of my generation across America were leaving their fields and factories, their offices and college campuses, their homes and farms, to do what needed to be done. It's history now. But at the time, it turned our lives upside-down.

After all of this one could naturally ask, "What did you get out of these undergraduate years at Berkeley?" My answer is short and simple—a good swift kick in the pants, which changed me from a lackadaisical, quiet kid into an alert, wanting-to-learn student, keen on finding out everything the university had to offer and determined to do what was necessary to cross the finish line with all the others. But Berkeley had to wait until we got back from a war.

GOOGLE GUIDE

Chapter 11: A Prisoner in a Chinese Cookie Factory

For more on this subject, try these:

"WWII – Day of Infamy – Japan Bombs Pearl Harbor." (film). Time: 7:57 min. Find title at YouTube: http://www.youtube.com/

"Edward R, Murrow from London -1942." (audio). http://www.archive.org/details/murrow_in_london_1942/

"Troop Train (1943)." (U.S. government film). http://www.archive.org/details/TroopTra1943/

For a longer listing, go to the book's web site:

Google Brain Book: http://googlebrainbook.blogspot.com/

Chapter 12

A Movie They Didn't Want Us to See

If the war didn't happen to kill you, it was bound to start you thinking.

George Orwell (1903-1950)

Note: The author was hospitalized while serving as a private in the 405th Infantry of the 102nd Division in World War II and not expected to live. After being given the last rites by a Catholic chaplain, he finally recovered, was transferred to Headquarters Company at Fort Dix, N. J., and assigned to the camp newspaper. He recalls the following:

It wasn't my fault they had to call out the military police. Nor could I blame New York newspaper columnist Ed Sullivan for what happened. Both of us were simply reporting the truth. Yet it led to hundreds of excited soldiers nearly causing a riot at Fort Dix, N.J., in January 1946, as they scrambled to get inside Post Theater No. 5 to see a new movie called *Scarlet Street*. Why such a fever to see an offbeat black and white movie? *Scarlet Street* certainly was not going to be the next *Gone With the Wind*.

Hollywood had made plenty of movies showing drunken sailors or soldiers needing to be controlled by MPs because they had consumed too much alcohol. But nobody could blame booze for this surprising episode. These GIs were serious minded and sober. They were angry about what they'd read in the *New York Daily News* and the *Fort Dix (N.J.) Post* about the movie being banned by the censors.

That irritated lots of men who had just returned from war, fighting to keep America a place where they could make up their own minds about such things in a free society. Let me set the scene for you: World War II was finally over. Most of the men—and women, too—at Fort Dix were about to be discharged in just a few days and would return to their homes in New York and other cities on the East Coast.

These were their final days of military service, and they were spending them at the largest separation center in the country, Fort Dix, where three thousand soldiers were being processed every day for civilian life. So why would these men and women risk jeopardizing their honorable discharge from military service over a movie? Why couldn't they just wait a few days to see this movie in their hometowns? The answer was simple: Unless they were able to see this film at Post Theater No. 5, they might never see it anywhere! They had read in their own post newspaper that the movie had been censored in New York, so it might never get to their hometowns. It had become a matter of principle.

When the word got around, they overwhelmed the system. Such vast numbers of GIs showed up to see this new Hollywood film that the auditorium filled up right away. The staff sergeant who managed the theater had to close the doors and turn away the pressing crowd outside, afraid the soldiers would force their way in and exceed the theater's capacity. He couldn't risk violating the fire code by packing more patrons inside.

When he finally called the MPs for help, he knew they would have a job on their hands quelling the potential melee. But many of the MPs were war veterans themselves. So they didn't bang any heads or arrest anyone unnecessarily, understanding the anger of the recently returned veterans from Europe and Asia, who had risked their lives overseas fighting for freedom.

At the time, I was a staff sergeant, editing the weekly camp newspaper, the *Fort Dix Post,* and also doing some radio work in its adjacent studios, WDIX. I headed a staff composed mostly of veterans of overseas service, many of whom had been reporters and photographers on New York and Philadelphia newspapers. We were always on the lookout for a front-page news story or a good feature story that would appeal to our readers.

Ordinarily it was a routine job to tell readers what movies were to be shown around the camp. We had six theaters, not counting those at our Army hospital. But the item I prepared about *Scarlet Street* was different. What led to my publicizing this unique story is that I happened to pick up a copy of the *New York Daily News* and spotted a small item in Ed Sullivan's gossip column saying that the New York State Motion Picture Commission had banned a movie called *Scarlet Street.*

When I found this out, I gave it a prominent spot on the front page of our Army camp newspaper. You couldn't miss the story's headline, which looked like something from *Variety,* the entertainment weekly: NY NIXES FLICK. The news account itself was a small, short feature, neatly boxed, and set in bold face, so that it hit readers smack dab in the face.

Before joining the Army, I had lived all my life in California and never heard of movie censorship anywhere in our land. However, when I first learned of it I was a U.S. Army soldier at a theater in Columbus, Ohio, seeing to my surprise an announcement flashed on the screen that this movie officially had been "approved by censors." It was peculiar, I thought, that a patriotic movie like *Casablanca* had to get official approval from a censorship board to be seen in Ohio. Later I was startled to see similar censorship notices attached to films being shown to audiences in other cities and states.

What was the reason *Scarlet Street* was now provoking the censors in New York? It was a routine B-movie thriller by Fritz Lang, the famous German director, who had escaped to America when the Nazis took over his homeland. While still in Germany, he had been acclaimed for making several great films, one of them being the powerful silent picture *Metropolis,* and the other, the equally impressive sound film called *M.* In America, he'd become known for making dark, shadowy thrillers like *Fury, You Only Live Once,* and *Man Hunt.*

This director's newest picture starred Edward G. Robinson as a timid, law-abiding citizen who is led astray by a conniving young woman, played by Joan Bennett. She not only seduces him but also leads him into criminal activity. When *Scarlet Street* came along, censors began sharpening their cutting scissors. The New York Motion Picture Division banned it from being shown on January 4, 1946. Ordinarily the practice of this censorship board was to simply cut and slash portions of pictures. But this time it banned the entire film. The 1921 statute allowed board members to tamper with any picture they deemed "obscene, indecent, immoral, inhuman, and sacrilegious" or that would "corrupt morals or incite to crime."

It outraged me to think that a handful of bureaucrats had been given such absolute power and that movie freedom had been taken away from ordinary American citizens. We had fought a war against dictatorship. Now veterans whose homes were in New York were forbidden to see this picture after fighting for constitutional democracy all over the world. Why didn't the First Amendment to the U.S. Constitution protect us against this abuse of power?

Several years later I would pursue the answer to this same question before the U.S. Supreme Court. But for the time being—as things eventually turned out— I gave a lot of veterans the chance to see the picture which had been banned in New York. Universal Pictures needed the New York market. It was the single largest movie market in the nation.

So it was the one million dollars spent to make the picture—not the First Amendment—that prompted Universal studios to send the film's executive producer, Walter Wanger, to New York to lobby for the film's release. Over the next few weeks Wanger, who was married to the film's leading lady Joan Bennett, met with the head of the Catholic Legion of Decency, key state officials, and others with powerful influence in government. After weeks of artful negotiation, Wanger won his points, got the film released, and *Scarlet Street* finally opened to its first New York audiences near Times Square (Loew's Criterion) on February 20. Today it's considered as a classic film noir achievement of director Fritz Lang and screenwriter Dudley Nichols.

When I remembered this personal experience several years later, I chose movie censorship as the topic for my master's thesis at the University of Minnesota and helped a New York attorney prepare a case for movie freedom before the U.S. Supreme Court. But credit for alerting us to the problem should go to Ed Sullivan, not because he eventually became a star of his own CBS television program, but for alerting us to the fact *Scarlet Street* was being banned.

As things turned out, Sullivan presented his first "really big show" to hundreds of veterans at an army post at the end of World War II and he didn't even know it.

GOOGLE GUIDE

Chapter 12: A Movie They Didn't Want Us to See

For more on this subject, try these:

"Scarlet Street (1945)." (Universal feature length film). Time: 102 min. http://www.archive.org/details/ScarletStreet/

"History Detectives, Blue Print Special." (Gordon Greb on PBS). http://www.pbs.org/opb/historydetectives/investigations/610bluepr intspecial.html

"Bonhoeffer: Jamming the wheels of the Nazi war machine." (film). 10:03 min. Find title at YouTube: http://www.youtube.com/

For a longer listing, go to the book's web site:

Google Brain Book: http://googlebrainbook.blogspot.com/

PART II

THE PROUD EGO

*The worst egoist is the person to whom
the thought has never occurred that he might be*

——Sigmund Freud (1856-1939)

Chapter 13

Homecoming

*I think that people want peace so much that one of these days
governments had better get out of the way and let them have it.*

——General Dwight D. Eisenhower (1890-1969)

I must been dreaming because the other morning I woke up thinking
about Wally. I'd been watching the last episode of Ken Burns' fifteen-
hour long television series, *The War*, the night before, and visual images
still lingered in my mind. They brought back memories of my brother
Wally and other kids from our high school who had fought in the
war.

I was standing at the wind-swept pier on the sunny San Francisco
docks, scanning the dark muddy waters of the bay for a glimpse of the
troop transport, with plenty of time to think. Lots of it. Long moments
to wonder what he'd look like after being gone three years, how he
made out on Okinawa and Korea, what he'd seen in the Pacific, and
what he probably wanted to forget. He was coming home.

We knew my brother and his outfit were aboard the incoming vessel,
the *Marine Devil*. Newspapers notified us of its expected arrival time a
week before. But nobody knew the exact debarkation plans for all the
men on board. The ship had been waiting patiently in San Francisco
Bay for a week until quarantine was lifted. According to the grapevine,
the ship was to pull up to the dock at 3 o'clock this afternoon.

So we all rushed to the far-end of the long docks and stood there,
waiting for it to tie up. Because few transports had been delayed so

long as this one to unload their human cargoes, it was difficult to be just hanging around and have nothing to do except stare at a slow, gray ship edging closer to the pier. But during the wait I had time to think. Groups of anxious onlookers were on the dock that day. Some were officers from Camp Stoneman, who like us were shifting nervously from one foot to another, waiting for their new arrivals. Others from the Presidio and regional naval command were on hand as well.

The vessel was coming closer now, moving slowly in the direction of the deep-water port. Then a truck screeched to a stop, and a driver hopped out quickly to drop the rear gate. Out tumbled a contingent of Women's Army Corps members, loaded down with musical instruments, the sun bouncing off their metal and sending out sharp reflections in all directions. The WACs assembled in front of the pier and swung into a snappy military march. No, it wasn't exactly a march. It was as if they were jiving to one of John Philip Souza's big numbers to welcome the boys home. The ship was sliding closer to the pier now, jam-packed with men looking over the side, staring down at the civilians ashore, searching faces for someone they knew.

We looked up. Too many soldier faces to pick out the one you knew, but you searched anyway. Maybe, just by accident, you could see him. The band music floated up from the sharp sea air. A mass of faces grinned back at us from the vessel. The sights and sounds of the pier must have seemed mighty good to them, plenty good, because what was happening was an undeniable fact. It was their real homecoming. A dream-come-true rushing up to meet them from stateside.

That's when I heard someone by my side remark, "Well, their morale looks pretty good." I turned to look at the man who'd uttered this pointless observation. He was decked out in a blue serge suit. "Brother," I thought to myself. "If you'd been overseas for two or three years, coming home now, your morale would be more than pretty good!"

Then a loud little donkey engine chugged into view, drowning out the conversation. It began hoisting a long gangplank to the side of the vessel. This was followed by the noise of a loudspeaker blaring aboard the ship, ordering men below deck to get ready for debarkation. Slowly the men disappeared from the railings on deck as they hurried below to get their gear. Only a few faces peered down on us now. Sailors on board were busily engaged tying the ramp to the ship, while officers from the receiving camp waited impatiently for word to go aboard.

Time passed slowly. It seemed like everything was going in slow motion. The ship had reached the Golden Gate and passed under that great bridge just 24 hours ahead of a tidal wave sweeping across the Pacific. Upon arrival, the ship, crew, and everyone aboard found themselves placed in quarantine for a week— right in San Francisco Bay, a stone's throw from home. Well, not exactly home, but their arrival city represented real terra ferma, its tall buildings, foggy mists, and funny-looking cable cars being home, in theory, to every man aboard.

Whether they came from Boston or Miami, New Orleans or Minneapolis, Omaha or Austin, Seattle or Los Angeles, this was home! Their suntanned faces began to appear on deck again, bulky bags slung over their shoulders, souvenir weapons poking odd shapes in their bags, and heavy loads weighing down on their backs.

Then word came from an officer holding a clipboard that he was ready to start reading names from the roster he held in his hand. Conversation stopped as he began announcing each name, calling them out, one by one.

"Ackerman, Akoury, Alfonso …"

They struggled down the steep-pitched ramp, first a long-legged Texan with a surprised look on his face, followed by a short fat guy who puffed coming down as fast as he could go, but happy at the effort. One man after another was now smiling from ear to ear, their grins getting wider as each foot pounded on solid, good old American wood. Wood that was sunk deep into good old American soil. They weren't afraid to say what they were thinking. This was something they had been dreaming about for a long time. Now it was really happening, as real as the heavy barracks bag they carried on their shoulders, easily now, lighter now, as the realization came this was the answer to a personal RSVP.

One blonde-headed veteran couldn't say anything more than "oh, boy … oh, boy" over and over again after he hit the dock. Another man twisted his neck around to squint at his wristwatch and just as his foot smacked the solid dock, he shouted, "4:50 and thirty-seconds. Those are numbers I'm never ever going to forget." Another just hollered,

"Whoopee." Some guys just widened their smiles. Others poked the man in front of them. "What do you say now, Joe! Ain't this what we dreamed of?"

I sensed the same feeling in each man, only expressed differently, one after another— an exuberant feeling for something that they'd wished and hoped for over too long a time. That's when I nearly choked on a piece of gum I was chewing. There he was—loping down the gangplank— that Oakland brother of mine. I'd know him anywhere, that happy, six-foot guy, that palooka I hadn't seen since using my own three-day pass to see him briefly three years ago on the East Coast where he had been training. Then suddenly, here he was at last, grabbing my hand, and saying something but I don't know exactly what. I was too excited. It was too good to be true.

My brother, Wallace, was home. He had been an eighteen-year old kid when I last saw him at Aberdeen Proving Grounds in Maryland, training to be a combat engineer. Since then he had been shipped to the Pacific, survived the invasion of Okinawa, the occupation of Korea, and the terrible possibility of invading Japan. Mom stood on her tiptoes to reach up and kiss his checks, filled with loving emotion, and my proud father pumped his son's hand to express his congratulations. I waited patiently for another chance and then gave him another firm welcome embrace.

Our experience wasn't unusual. Ask returning veterans of any war, anytime, and anyplace to name the happiest moment in life. I'll bet it would have been something just like this! Wally rarely talked about what happened over there and that was like a lot of other war veterans who were only too glad that particular part of their life was finally over. In the years that followed, Wally's was a happy one. But this night, as I lay dreaming of his homecoming, it all came back to me and I, too, was glad it was over.

GOOGLE GUIDE

Chapter 13: Homecoming

For more on this subject, try these:

"21 Nazi Chiefs Guilty, Nuremberg Trials 1946/10/8." (newsreel). Time: 4:46 min. Find title at YouTube: http://www.youtube.com/

"The USO Honors the Military as told by Bob Hope." (film). Find title at YouTube: http://www.youtube.com/

"The Further Adventures of Rusty, Boy Aviator: April 4, 2005," by Gordon Greb. (column). http://www.thecolumnists.com/greb/greb14.html/

For a longer listing, go to the book's web site:

Google Brain Book: http://googlebrainbook.blogspot.com/

Chapter 14

Where Do We Go From Here?

I want a future that will live up to my past.

——Alan Bennett (1934-)

The war was over! Japan had surrendered! President Truman took to the airwaves and made it official on August 14, 1945. And with the knowledge that Germany already had capitulated months earlier on May 8, we now knew for certain this was it. We had peace at last! But for me and thousands of others, the question was, "What happens next?"

The joy and relief of the war's ending is impossible to describe today. But you can still feel much of that day's emotions on audio recordings of the excited and happy crowds that jammed the streets around Piccadilly Circus in London, Times Square in New York City, or the Ferry Building in San Francisco. While movies today can show you these celebrants and their happy faces, you need to hear a playback of the actual sounds made on that day to really get the feel of it.

The end of hostilities was wildly welcomed everywhere but especially overseas by men and women in uniform. Millions of soldiers, sailors, marines, and airmen cheered, laughed, and sang on hearing the news. Word spread swiftly from place to place by radio and telephone, newspaper and telegraph. It swept across Europe, the Americas, Pacific, and Asia to wherever they were stationed. And the next day, the amazing reality of what had happened struck twelve million young Americans scattered all over the world—at last they were coming home! After three years in the U.S. Army that same thought also occurred to me.

While I had to wait my turn and it was six more months longer before it actually happened, I finally got my Honorable Discharge papers at Fort Dix, N.J. in the spring of 1946, said goodbye to all my friends around New York City, and started a five-day journey by train across the country to California. Still wearing my uniform when I left Grand Central station, I joined a trainload of other servicemen and women, deliriously happy to be heading west and going home.

Mingling with passengers on the Union Pacific's *City of San Francisco* out of Chicago, I found that nearly everyone on board had a story to tell. I talked to a parachute veteran of the 82nd Airborne; another soldier who had been protecting the Panama Canal; and an older civilian, a scientist, who had helped develop the A-bomb at the University of Chicago.

What pleased me most was that train would our stop at North Platte, Nebraska, and the happy discovery that the station canteen was still open and being run by those same wonderful volunteers, groups of women who treated us as though we were sons and daughters of their own. Throughout the war, these mothers, wives, daughters, and sisters of middle America had met every troop train passing through and greeted everyone in uniform with free offerings of cake, sandwiches, and doughnuts as though we members of their own families. Remarkably, these lovely ladies sacrificed portions of their own rationed food for us boys.

When we finally arrived at Oakland, my dad met me with a big smile on his face, tossed my luggage into his 1934 Ford, and suggested we stop at a nearby restaurant for some coffee and doughnuts. "It's great to see you back, son," he said happily. "I suppose you'll need some time to figure out what to do next?" Well, yes, I agreed that was something I'd been thinking about for quite awhile. I told him that I'd made one crucial decision already, saying, "One of my army buddies, Sergeant Jack Israel, offered me a job in his advertising agency in Philadelphia. It was a great offer and I almost took it. But—well, here I am—back home."

Now amidst familiar surroundings, everything seemed to fall naturally into place and to return to normal. After three years of having had my life run by the army and someone else telling me what to do, I wondered when I'd start thinking for myself. Oddly enough, nothing seemed particularly difficult at the moment. Thanks to the GI Bill, I had no problem returning to the University of California at Berkeley to complete my undergraduate degree. As for getting my job back as a reporter for the *San Leandro News-Observer* and teaming up with Dave Houser to resume radio newscasting again over KROW, Oakland, I found nothing to bar my way, and I began picking up my life where I'd left off.

By the time 1946 was over, I was ready to launch a full-time career. But what was it to going to be? Having chosen to become a writer, I still couldn't decide between newspapers, public relations, advertising, magazines, or radio. Frankly I have no idea why making this decision seemed so important, but I was now twenty-five years old and couldn't afford to make a false start. One night at home I sat down at my desk, got out a clean piece of paper, and began evaluating what I hoped to accomplish in life.

It was clear that I needed to undertake an honest self-analysis to avoid the wrong decision. I knew it would be a mistake to accept the first job that came along and find out later I was stuck in a dead-end career. Whether this meticulous examination of my talents, experiences, likes and dislikes, sorted things out properly, and actually pointed me in the right direction, I really don't know. But here are some of the things that came to my mind at the time.

For a kid who grew up in the Great Depression, the big money possibilities in advertising and public relations had vast appeal. But in 1946 I saw Clark Gable in the role of an account executive in a Hollywood movie, *The Hucksters,* based on a book by Frederic Wakeman. It was a devastating expose and made a strong impression on my mind. Its depiction of the worst practices and temptations of Madison Avenue left me convinced me that I'd be miserable spending a lifetime trying to sell toothpaste, mouthwash, or cigarette brands. So I said, "No thanks," and walked away from a chance to work for the McCann-Erickson advertising agency in San Francisco.

Since magazine writing called for a lot of creativity, it had a strong appeal. I'd long admired the short story writing of O. Henry, who first appeared in *McClure's* magazine and was popular for years afterward. Cartooning took me to *The New Yorker* where I discovered the humor of Robert Benchley, James Thurber, and Dorothy Parker. I'd already begun earning extra money by selling pieces to a few national magazines and received an "A" in magazine writing in a course I'd just taken at UC Berkeley. So why not try freelance writing? But rejection slips from *The Saturday Evening Post, Liberty,* and *Colliers* soon told me that freelancing was an uphill climb and precarious for a beginner.

So I rejected this option in favor of a more certain and secure occupation. Newspaper reporting and editing was what I'd studied in college. I liked the fact that reporters were eyewitnesses to history, covered some of the most exciting issues and people of the day, and contributed to democratic government by keeping the people informed. The press had the power to change things, and a reporter had access to nearly everyone, from the lowest to the mightiest, simply by showing his press credentials.

I admired honest journalism whether by conservatives like William Allen White, publisher of the *Emporia Gazette*, who woke up the Republican Party with his editorial, "What's the Matter with Kansas?" or the liberal reporting of Lincoln Steffens, who helped inspire a reform movement in his *The Shame of the Cities* and *The Struggle for Self-Government.*

In the final analysis, I decided on radio. Twisting the dial to find interesting stations on the air was like searching on the Internet today. From one end of the spectrum to the next, a grand variety of fascinating shows awaited the listener—music, drama, comedy, talks, games, news, weather, speeches, and a lot more. Radio was what I liked to do, because it involved so many things—news, music, interviews, documentaries, and drama.

Beginning in 1939 I'd begun recording short-wave wave programs from overseas, including propaganda broadcasts from England, Germany, and Japan. I heard CBS carrying the latest news from Edward R. Murrow in London and William L. Shirer in Berlin, and I wanted to be there. But all I had to offer as experience was a short stint as a child actor on KTAB, weekly newscasts on KROW, and occasional producing at WDIX at Fort Dix. Would that be enough to get me a full-time job in broadcasting?

Looking around for some more rigorous kind of guidance I turned to the results of a Strong Vocational Interest Test, which I'd taken twice in psychology courses, once before the war and more recently in Professor Edward Tolman's course on "Motivational Analysis" at Berkeley. My test scores came out practically the same each time. My top scores pointed to a career in public administration, music, and teaching and the next best numbers to jobs like those of a journalist, policeman, or secretary of a non-profit organization.

I took all of these results into consideration in finally deciding where to aim my ambitions. It occurred to me there was no sense going to college, if you simply dismissed out of hand what you worked hard to learn. Professor E.K. Strong, whose testing methods continue to be applied today, had theorized as far back as the 1920s that the closer your interests matched those in various occupations, the better your chances of succeeding.

Then I got a phone call from my friend Dave Houser, who luckily had been assigned to Armed Forces Radio in Europe during the last year of the war and now had found a job in radio. "I've been hired to help put a new FM station on the air—KRCC—owned and operated by the *Richmond Daily Independent*. I've talked to the general manager and he said he could use you. Of course, you won't be paid right away but he said it would be great experience."

I jumped at the chance, hopped into the car, and drove to KRCC's hilltop studios overlooking San Francisco Bay. There I was taught everything General Manager Phil Bernheim knew about radio—how to write commercial copy, type up logs, feed a news wire, script programs, select music, and run a control board—which at the time was not being taught in college. Soon I was a disc jockey spinning records on the air and reading news off the United Press wire.

A month later I had no hesitancy assuring a future employer, "Yes sir, I can do it because that's what I've been doing at KRCC." That's how I broke into broadcasting and stayed with it for the rest of my life. I began working as a reporter for the *San Rafael Independent-Journal*, until the new station it owned got on the air in the spring of 1947. The publisher Roy Brown and Station Manager Ernie Smith were impressed by what I had been doing at KRCC-FM and liked the fact

I could write. So they had me handling newspaper assignments before taking over as news director for the new station, KTIM.

I hesitate to recount much more. It brings to mind what happened years later at a meeting of *Broadcast Legends* in San Francisco when the program chairman Norm Howard introduced me by reading off the call letters of all the stations with which I'd been affiliated.

It was a long list that included radio stations KTAB, KROW, KRCC, KTIM, KVSM, KLX, KUOM, KRNO, KOAC, KNX, KSJO, KSJS and television stations KNTV-TV, KABC-TV, KNBC-TV, KQED-TV, KCSM-TV, and KTEH-TV."

After a pause, he looked at me and said, "Wow! This guy can't hold a job."

GOOGLE GUIDE

Chapter 14: Where Do We Go From Here?

For more on this subject, try these:

"Broadway 1950s New York City at Night." (film).
Find title at YouTube: http://www.youtube.com/

"Teletours San Francisco 1950 Man on the Street." (film).
Find title at YouTube: http://www.youtube.com/

"Broadcast Legends Membership Roster, Gordon Greb." (biography).
http://www.BroadcastLegends.com/

For a longer listing, go to the book's web site:

Google Brain Book: http://googlebrainbook.blogspot.com/

Chapter 15

My Own Fight with McCarthyism

Mr. Hammett, if you were in our position, would you allow your book in the United States Information Service libraries?

——Senator Joe McCarthy, chairman of committee

If I were you, Senator, I would not allow any libraries.

——Dashiell Hammett (1894-1961)

What is it that defines Edward R. Murrow? The answer given me by former radio and television newsman Marvin Kalb, now teaching at Harvard in a special communications program, hardly came as a surprise. In correspondence with Kalb, I ended my message saying, "Good night and good luck," which was the way Murrow ended his reports during the London blitz in the Second World War.

Kalb knew the point I was trying to make, saying, "Thanks, for I shall remember those words and ERM for as long as I live." Hollywood had saluted Murrow in 2005 with a well-received feature film, *Good Night and Good Luck,* a title taken from Murrow's famous wartime shortwave reports. The film was nominated for the Best Picture Academy Award and was on nearly everyone's Ten Best List. It was Murrow who had revealed that broadcasting could be a real service to society.

Actor-writer George Clooney and the film's other producers, writers, directors and actors did well to bring Murrow to life for a new generation. We constantly need to be reminded of the crises newsmen face. The public needs to know that journalists conscientiously want the truth and will endure tremendous difficulties in trying to achieve it. If the Murrow film encourages more in the media to stand up to today's challenges and take a stand for freedoms, we will be the better for it.

I was as proud as a peacock working as a newsman at CBS West Coast headquarters in Los Angeles in the summer of 1951. Six months earlier I'd driven to Southern California to make a wonderful young kindergarten teacher named Darlene Alcock my bride over Christmas vacation and celebrate our honeymoon by driving back to Eugene, Oregon, where I was teaching at the University of Oregon. I'd been teaching in the School of Journalism and had found a little cottage for us to live in near the university.

While I loved living among the picturesque mountains, woods, and streams of the state, I came to realize that the region's chilly climate and constant rain was having a deleterious effect on my new wife, who grew up in Southern California. Shortly after we moved into our cottage opposite the football stadium, a huge flood engulfed the neighboring city of Springfield and was driving hundreds from their homes. When the job at CBS opened up, it couldn't have arrived at a more opportune time. I accepted and returned to California.

CBS definitely was my place and time. This network had become a powerful force under the influence of Edward R. Murrow. It was building one of the greatest news organizations in the world, and I was part of it. As Steve Allen, then one of my fellow staffers, once put it, "This could be the start of something big." We both were at the CBS flagship station KNX, Hollywood, and he later became a shining light and national celebrity on television's *Tonight Show.*

Although Murrow worked out of Manhattan, he was the broadcast journalist who had influenced me more than anyone else. I had made it a practice to study his programs and scripts in my work as well as my teaching, hoping his high standards would be those of our entire profession. Although colleagues in Los Angeles urged me to move to New York, News Director Jack Beck told me, "You're one of the best men in my newsroom and I want you to stay here." He further inflated my ego saying, "I've had writers here from *The New Yorker* not as good as you." With that praise, it's no wonder I felt a great career was at hand.

By good fortune, my friend Sig Mickelson, who had once offered me a job in the newsroom at WCCO in Minneapolis, was now president of CBS News. Because television was in its infancy, new positions were opening up, and I was on the ground floor with excellent prospects. But the one thing I hadn't expected was casting its shadow over the newsroom—the growing anxiety over communism and our country's decision on how best to fight it domestically. Soon McCarthyism would force me to choose.

There was good reason for concern. Peace and security was being threatened worldwide. The U.S.S.R had tried to isolate and seize West Berlin with a blockade in 1948 and President Truman broke it with a courageous airlift. China had been taken over by communists in 1949 and would confront us in Korea. We went to war to save South Korea in 1950, but that conflict was still going on a year later.

At home spies Julius and Ethel Rosenberg were found guilty of passing atomic bomb secrets to the Soviet Union and were now sentenced to death. U.S. courts were sending dozens of Communist Party leaders to prison for conspiring to overthrow the U.S. government by force and violence. General Dwight D. Eisenhower was leading a new alliance of free nations (NATO) in Europe against a militant eastern bloc of communists. The threat of communism was not illusionary. But how should we deal with it here at home?

I had resigned a faculty position at the University of Oregon to take the job at CBS that summer, elated to be joining such a great news organization. But I had no idea when my wife and I moved to Southern California that CBS owner-executive William S. Paley, afraid of losing sponsors, wanted everyone to sign a loyalty oath. So a week after I arrived at Columbia Square, I was handed a lot of papers to sign, which at first seemed like a simple formality.

It didn't surprise me that CBS wanted rights to everything I invented or created on the job, but what astonished me was this attempt to deny me my right to keep my political opinions to myself. After due deliberation, I refused to sign the CBS oath and offered one of my own to take its place—a statement pledging to defend and protect the Constitution of the United States and Bill of Rights against all enemies, both foreign and domestic, which is what I had done as a soldier in World War II.

This was nearly identical to the oath that the U.S. President and other high-ranking office holders take, sometimes with their hand on a Bible, on assuming the responsibilities of office. As veteran of World War II, someone who had been honorably discharged from the U.S. Army after three years of service, I thought CBS had plenty of evidence of my loyalty. The fact was that I had nothing to hide, politically or otherwise, and took my stand for the very reason that I had an obligation to defend the constitution.

I found CBS ignorant of the law. Its oath requirement did not contain a "knowingly" clause. Too many innocent people had unwittingly signed petitions or stumbled into suspect organizations because they thought they were supporting worthy causes, unaware of the true nature of the organization sponsoring them. Although they had exercised their rights as citizens, they had not, in fact, "knowingly" joined any particular group and should not be held accountable for that. In addition, CBS was requiring its employees to deny they had been associated with any organizations deemed subversive by the U. S. Attorney General and attached a list of names of all the government objected to. Another court case had ruled that action contrary to law.

I could have easily signed the oath and kept my job at CBS West Coast News headquarters at KNX, Columbia Square, Hollywood. But I felt that in so doing I would be deserting friends I knew on the faculty and respected at the University of California at Berkeley, who were opposing the oath as a violation of the Bill of Rights. To my mind, it was a dangerous and ineffective move to suppress opinion, as anyone planning to subvert our society would sign a loyalty oath in order not to be exposed. To my mind it was an oath the courts eventually would find violated my fundamental rights as an American citizen. But as I had little money in the bank and was only recently married (six months earlier), I was in no position to pay the costs of challenging the matter in court myself.

It was a hard decision to make because everything pointed to my having a promising career at CBS had I stayed. But I did it. Thankfully my new bride Darlene, who incidentally came from a very conservative family, said she would support me—not only morally but also financially—since she could return to teaching kindergarten. So we both decided it was necessary for me to take a stand and live by my convictions.

Secure in what my father had taught me, who had been a strong believer in our American democratic government, I held to these fundamental beliefs from childhood. In college I was surprised to find history professors requiring us to read both the *U.S. Constitution* as well as Marx's *Communist Manifesto* to be properly educated. It then dawned on me that these professors knew and believed that Americans, especially their young students, could be trusted to be exposed to the ideas of foreign ideology so long as they knew the strengths of their own.

In the days and weeks that followed my refusal to sign the conformity oath, I was asked to see more and more important people higher up in the network. Gradually I worked my way up the chain of command to the vice president on the West Coast. While I had no way of knowing that Edward R. Murrow had, in fact, signed the CBS oath and urged others to follow his lead to implement a plan of his own, but I did learn later that the network had fired no one who had admitted some kind of previous political indiscretion. Because I had nothing to hide, this argument by the CBS vice president in Los Angeles carried little weight with me. So the New York office made the decision for him—the network let me go.

It pleased me greatly at the time and still does today that I had great support from my colleagues. News Director Beck not once doubted my loyalty. Before I left, he assigned me to cover a super-secret national defense program. With a CBS engineer recording my questions, I spoke up at a press conference with General Albert E. Wedemeyer, who had recently been made head of a classified project called VISTA. It turned out that his answer to my question became the "lead" for the *Los Angeles Times'* coverage, the wire services, and the CBS network for the next 24 hours.

One week before my dismissal I was promoted to the position of CBS West Coast News Editor and was told I could return to the network anytime I was willing to sign the objectionable oath. Instead I left for Stanford University to begin studies for a doctorate in political science, which I believed would confirm my understanding of constitutional law. Among Stanford students who shared the law library with me about the same time, although we never met, were Sandra Day (O'Connor) and William Rehnquist, both of whom would be appointed later to the U.S. Supreme Court.

What finally helped to end McCarthyism was the exemplary use of television by the CBS news organization—Murrow's shattering exposure of the senator, depicted in Clooney's new movie—and the Army-McCarthy hearings. Years later the question was resolved. The oath itself was tested in the American judicial system and declared unconstitutional.

CBS finally made its amends in 1959 when I did the network a favor. I had researched the origins of radio, found that broadcasting had originated in San Jose in 1909, and that the station was now owned by CBS in San Francisco. This prompted CBS radio network president Arthur Hull Hayes to fly out to California to help us celebrate the fiftieth anniversary of broadcasting, accompanied by network stars to help salute it worldwide on the network. At an awards ceremony on April 2, 1959, I was presented with a plaque which read: "KCBS Radio Commends Gordon Greb, Assistant Professor, San Jose State College, for Establishing KCBS as the First Radio Broadcasting Station in the World."

As I happily associated with these CBS executives, who were praising me for my work, I sometimes wondered, "Does anyone at the network know that they once fired me?" A few years later I had the privilege of meeting Ed Murrow in Washington, D.C. and was glad to shake his hand. As Murrow helped defeat McCarthyism in his own way, I often wonder whether my stand wasn't valuable, too. He stayed at CBS to fight McCarthyism on the job, while I left to study constitutional law at Stanford. Maybe we both talked sense to those who would listen in our own ways?

What finally counted for me was the fact my wife, friends and family stuck by me throughout the whole experience.

GOOGLE GUIDE

Chapter 15: My Own Fight With McCarthyism

For more on this subject, try these:

"The Tennessee Waltz – Singer Patti Page 1950." (song).
Find title at YouTube: http://www.youtube.com/

"Edward R. Murrow." (film). Time: 6:21 min.
Find title at YouTube: http://www.youtube.com/

"Undefeated and Uninvited." (film). Time: 2:30 min.
Find title at YouTube: http://www.youtube.com/

For a longer listing, go to the book's web site:

Google Brain Book: http://googlebrainbook.blogspot.com/

Chapter 16

Hollywood Finds a Miracle

*A censor is a man who knows more
than he thinks you ought to know.*

——Laurence J. Peter (1919-1920)

When I first thought of challenging movie censorship, experts on the subject told me it couldn't be done. The idea of making freedom of the movies my thesis topic came to me at the University of Minnesota in 1949 when I needed a subject to study and write about for my master's thesis.

Remembering years earlier being shocked to see feature films censored in states like Ohio, Pennsylvania, and New York, where I was stationed as a soldier in World War II, I decided the question was important to me as someone who firmly believed in the right of free speech and press. So I decided to take it on, basing my argument on the First Amendment to the U.S. Constitution. My reasoning was basically that movies should be as free as the print media throughout the United States of America.

That's when a visiting scholar, a professor from the University of Illinois, who was both a Ph.D. and an attorney, told me, "It can't be done. You'd be wasting your time choosing that for your subject because the U.S. Supreme Court allowed film censorship in 1915. That's a precedent which the high court has been following for years and your chances of overturning it are practically nil."

This should have stopped me dead in my tracks. It ought to have discouraged me from going further, because the thought passed through my mind, "Who am I to question what the greatest jurists in the land had decided?" After all, I was a mere graduate student, a fledging young journalist with no background in law other than a strong interest in freedom of speech and press. I could be wasting my time trying to win freedom for the movies and end up never finishing my master's degree by challenging something that already had been settled in law.

My purpose in becoming a graduate student at Minnesota in the first place was to study audience and public opinion measurement, which the school of journalism was noted for. It had bothered me as manager of the East Bay Studios of KVSM that I couldn't honestly answer some simple questions posed by potential advertisers, which were: "Who listens to your station? What's the size of your audience?"

So I left radio temporarily to learn how to do scientific survey research, choosing by happenstance the most opportune time. It was 1948, the year the polls got it wrong in the presidential election. Overnight the weakness in methodology was identified and we began learning the correct techniques. Thus my original goal was not in vain because I did use what I learned about polling techniques on returning to California.

However, I was not enthused about making survey research the subject for my thesis. Being young, stubborn, and a citizen who believed the U.S. Constitution stood for freedom of the press, I felt government censorship had no place in a free society. Common sense told me the word "press" as understood in the eighteenth century should now include all forms of expression, whether by radio, recordings, telephone, public address systems, motion pictures, or at the time of my study, the newly developing television industry.

I knew from earlier study of constitutional law that the "commerce" clause of the U.S. Constitution had been interpreted widely since it was first written. According to the high court, it no longer was meant to cover merely the trading conditions of the horse and buggy days of the colonial era but also our more modern forms of exchanging goods and services, such as commerce conducted by means of railroad, motorcar, and airplane. Thus plain common sense told me the First Amendment should protect our newer media, too.

I had to admit it was risky taking on this project. Censors had withstood challenges to their authority for more than thirty years and everyone who ever tried to overturn film censorship from 1915 to 1948 had found the odds against him. Yet I filed the necessary forms with the School of Journalism at the University of Minnesota, allowing me to challenge the movie censorship question with my topic, "Freedom of the Movies to Present News and Opinions."

Whether it was the memory of having admired John Stuart Mill's great essay *On Liberty*, the advocacy of our rights as citizens by Clarence Darrow in the Scopes case, or the dramatization of Abraham Lincoln's respect for the constitution in movies starring Raymond Massey as *Lincoln of Illinois* (1940) or Henry Fonda in *Young Mr. Lincoln* (1939), I decided to take it on.

What I found in the University of Minnesota library confirmed what I'd been told. In the case of the *Mutual Film Corporation v. Industrial Commission of Ohio*, the U. S. Supreme Court had ruled that movies were a business for profit, not an art form, and therefore were not entitled to protection of the First Amendment.

In that unanimous 1915 decision, all nine justices declared movies were no more important than a "circus" or similar "spectacles." Speaking for the court, Mr. Justice McKenna declared that movies were made for profit and were not to be regarded as "part of the press of the country, or as organs of public opinion." Thus any city or state across the land could ban objectionable films through the exercise of their police power.

Empowered by the high court's 1915 ruling, censorship boards sprang up in Ohio, Kansas, New York, Maryland, Pennsylvania, Virginia, and Massachusetts. But soon there were unanticipated problems. Deletions of objectionable scenes by one state often affected what was seen in another. For example, Rhode Island, Vermont, and New Hampshire often saw movies that had been censored in Massachusetts. In one case alone, Massachusetts's scissored parts out of newsreels thirteen times during a one-year period, effectively deleting what audiences could see in neighboring states.

However, as I discovered in the literature that followed, there was a strong body of opinion among critics urging that the 1915 case be overturned. I found a wide range of opinion, varying from those of journalists to legal scholars, contending that movie censorship was wrong. But despite their objections, they failed to have this decision reversed. So I stuck with my decision to argue for movie freedom and began to laboriously assemble a factual argument that would prove my own logical and legal case of why this should be done.

Fortunately my course work had been completed by the summer of 1949. So I packed up my research materials, headed for the University of California at Berkeley to continue my research there, and then moved closer to the movie industry by accepting a teaching position at San Bernardino Valley College in Southern California. This was an ideal location. It gave me an easy commute to Hollywood and personal access to the archives and film library of the Academy of Motion Picture Arts and Sciences.

What I learned, of course, was that many of the early silent films were notoriously violent, brutish, and short. Filmmakers were eager to make money more than tell the truth. In the early days, some producers shot fake newsreels of Teddy Roosevelt's "Rough Riders" charging up San Juan Hill in the Spanish-American War and others lured Pancho Villa in Mexico with a twenty-five thousand dollar payoff to fight his battles in the daylight hours so that a film company could record the uprisings.

In the early days of the nickelodeon, many producers had little interest in Shakespeare and serious literature, preferring slapstick comedy that drew crowds. Fat and frustrated cops chased befuddled villains; moviegoers cringed in terror as they witnessed a railroad train headed down the track toward them; and as an editorial in the *Chicago Tribune* proclaimed, "they are hopelessly bad." But since this exploitation of the nonsensical and trivial opened the door to censorship, it set a pattern that would curb, confuse, and limit the industry for years to come.

When censorship laws were written, they were supposed to deal with what authorities considered immoral, degrading, or criminal. However, many board members interpreted the rules broadly and deleted whatever suited their fancy. For instance, the authority given to censors by the city ordinance of Memphis, Tennessee stated, "It shall be unlawful to exhibit any play, picture, pantomime … inimical to the public safety, health, and welfare." But when it was applied to Hal

Roach's comedy *Curley*, the film was banned on the grounds that white children should not be seen playing with Negro youngsters.

Films cut by censors in Kansas were often those distributed to audiences in Missouri. And audiences in West Virginia and Kentucky got movies sliced by Ohio. In the South, censors ruled against pictures that supported racial equality and consequently refused to allow their audiences to see *Pinky, Home of the Brave*, and *Lost Boundaries*.

By 1922 the clamor for censorship had reached such proportions that Hollywood industry leaders turned to self-regulation as a solution to their problems. They persuaded Postmaster General Will H. Hays to take charge of a new organization, the Motion Picture Producers and Distributors of America, and promised him a free hand in regulating content. This action came none too soon. Seven states had by this time enacted censorship laws and voters in other cities and states were being asked to approve censorship as well.

With Hays arguing for self-regulation of the movies and leading the fight against government intervention, censorship bills were defeated in thirty state legislatures. Congress was given 44 bills to regulate movies between 1924 and 1940 but failed to enact any. Hays, who served until 1945, said he hoped someday movies would be protected under the First Amendment.

As long as the 1915 decision hung over Hollywood, fear alone was pressure enough for some major studios to censor themselves. In 1937 a Paramount newsreel cameraman shot film of Chicago police charging strikers outside the Republic Steel Corporation, attacking these pickets with billy clubs, which provoked a riot. Despite the fact several workers and innocent bystanders were killed or injured by the police, Paramount decided not to release its film. Not until the LaFollette Civil Liberties Committee began an investigation were these newsreels ever shown on a screen. Chicago citizens had been barred from seeing police brutality taking place in their own city.

Since I had chosen to battle for motion picture freedom, I wondered about the attitude of the motion picture industry itself. So I surveyed key figures in Hollywood by sending out letters to representative leaders, asking them to comment. Each responded to my query and gave me their views on two basic questions:

(1) Do you think the motion picture should have the same freedom as the newspaper in presenting news and opinion and receive the protection of the First Amendment to the U.S. Constitution?

(2) Do you know of any cases of censorship of movies in presentation of news and/or opinions?

When the results from this survey came in, I was left with little doubt about where Hollywood stood. Well-known screenwriters, producers, directors, and studio heads overwhelmingly favored First Amendment protection; and one of the strongest replies came from a future president of the United States.

Ronald Reagan, president of the Screen Actors Guild: "The motion picture is a medium of expression, entertainment, opinion, and information. It is just as much so as the press and radio. If one medium of expression can be denied the full right of freedom of the press, then all mediums of expression can be denied that right. Censorship ... is a restraint of opinion which in itself is contrary to the very principles upon which this country was founded."

Dudley Nichols, winner of an Academy Award for scripting *The Informer* and former president of the Screen Writers Guild, gave me a statement, saying: "Of course film should be as free as any other form of expression and communication. And of course it is not ... I automatically know what cannot be done and what will get the studios in hot water ... But the fact is I am getting very weary of the film medium because of the increasingly limited areas of truth one can touch."

Dore Schary, vice president of Metro-Goldwyn-Mayer Studios: "First of all, let me say right away that I believe that film should enjoy all the prerogatives and privileges of the press ..."

Art Cohn, script writer, who air mailed his reply from the island of Stromboli where he was working on a film by the same name with Roberto Rossellini and Ingrid Berman, stated: "Do I think Hollywood ought to have the same privileges as the press in expression of opinions or taking sides in politics? Hell, yes. Fear is censorship's greatest ally. Hollywood is afraid, now more than ever, because the receipts are down. Politically, the screen is now a vacuum, a Sahara, and it will be for a long, long time ..."

Not only did this thesis easily earn me a master's degree but also it persuaded me to pursue doctoral studies in constitutional law at Stanford University. It was there that I read in the papers that on February 4, 1952, the U. S. Supreme Court had accepted a movie censorship case from New York and I immediately realized movie freedom could rise or fall on its outcome. So I decided to help.

The film's distributor Joseph Burstyn had lost the case in the lower court. He had tried to show a foreign film by Roberto Rossellini called *The Miracle* (originally *L'Amore* in Italian) and had been stopped by the New York censors. Since the high court had not taken a movie censorship case for thirty-seven years but had decided to do so now, I wrote Burstyn saying that I supported his case and offered to mail him my thesis. Quickly I heard from his attorney, Ephraim S. London of New York, who urged me to send him everything I had written, which I did. Then I heard nothing more till months later.

On May 26 I got a phone call from a reporter friend of mine, Ward Winslow of the *Palo Alto Times*, saying, "Greb, you've done it. The Supreme Court has ruled in your favor." Since we had known each other as newspapermen for some time, I had previously given Winslow some background of my involvement in the case and was anxious now to know everything about the court's ruling.

According to the first wire service report, this was a landmark decision and it got headlines nationally by completely overturning the old 1915 ruling. Writing on behalf of the U.S. Supreme Court, Mr. Justice Clark clearly explained what caused the justices to reach their unanimous decision (9 -0) in *Burstyn v. Wilson, et al.* It was principally that a motion picture like *The Miracle* could not be censored on basis of its being "sacrilegious." Six justices had joined Clark in taking the argument that movie censorship violated the First Amendment and its guarantees of free speech and press. The other three agreed, based on other points of law.

When the story about my role in the case broke on the front page of the *Palo Alto Times,* I was walking down the hallway at Stanford University when Dr. Thomas Barkley, professor of political science, saw me and said, "Mr. Greb, you're now as famous as Dred Scott." What especially pleased me most was the special praise I got from Dr. Charles

Fairman in my constitutional law class, who said, "I'd appreciate your allowing me to read you thesis someday, Mr. Greb."

When thanks arrived from the law offices of London and London in New York, the attorney who won the case, Ephraim S. London, said, "Your thesis was of considerable help and assistance," adding that "I am amazed that someone who is not a lawyer could have had so clear a comprehension of the legal questions involved."

As an example of how my research had helped, London said he had quoted my work in the oral argument before the justices to refute the claim that the movie industry favored licensing statutes.

Recalling how I assisted in the case, he wrote, "I therefore found it necessary, in my closing statement to the Court, to point out that the M.P.P.A. was sponsoring the Gelling case and that the leaders of the motion picture industry in the country had, on many occasions, as pointed out by you, advocated repeal of the licensing laws."

It was finally over. We had won. After years of struggling to be free, Hollywood had found its miracle. Now I could walk around like a peacock not worrying about being called Don Quixote tilting at windmills, because I was now, in fact, an honest-to-goodness guardian angel. And that's the kind of ending writers always like to imagine for their real-life Hollywood movies!

GOOGLE GUIDE

Chapter 16: Hollywood Finds a Miracle

For more on this subject, try these:

"The Professor's Reel Life," by Gordon Greb. (column).
http://www.thecolumnists.com/greb/greb65.html/

"Robert Benchley: Home Movies." (film).
Find title at YouTube: http://www.youtube.com/

"Children and the Movies: Media Influences and the Payne Fund Controversy," by Garth S. Jowett, Ian C. Jarvie, and Kathryn H. Fuller. (book).
Find title at Google Books: http://books.google.com/

For a longer listing, go to the book's web site:

Google Brain Book: http://googlebrainbook.blogspot.com/

Chapter 17

I Help Democrats Win

I have only one firm belief about the American political system, and that is this:God is a Republican and Santa Claus is a Democrat.

—P. J. O'Rourke (1947-)

I had no idea becoming a graduate student at Stanford University in 1951 would plunge me into liberal politics but it did. Getting some practical experience to balance out the classroom theory seemed like a good idea. However, if you consider yourself a conservative and this alarms you, please don't be put off by this liberal admission by tossing this book into the nearest wastebasket. I'm as much a conservative in many ways as I'm a moderate or a liberal.

Wasn't Abraham Lincoln a radical thinker when he opposed slavery? Wasn't Winston Churchill a left-of-center liberal when he supported old age benefits in England? Didn't Ronald Reagan strongly support Roosevelt's jobs program of the New Deal? Find out why they took the positions they did. Let's not allow the competition of ideas between donkeys and elephants in America to be reduced to a contest of meaningless and empty labels.

When I became eligible to vote at the age of twenty-one, I refused to join either major political party, preferring instead to think of myself as an independent. By registering as non-partisan, I figured it gave me the chance to choose among all the candidates and not those of any particular party.

However, California law at that time allowed for "cross-filing" by the candidates; that is, a person running for political office could seek both his own party nomination as well as that of the opposition. In practice this meant that when most people voted, the outcome tended to favor incumbents whose names were well known. Voters tended to be wary of political newcomers they'd never heard of.

When the results of the 1952 primary elections came in, I suddenly realized California was slowly turning into a one-party state. Contests were over before they started. One of the ways U.S. Senator William F. Knowland won reelection was by means of cross-filing, which allowed him to run in both major party primaries. On becoming the nominee of both parties, what were voters to think: was he actually a Republican or a Democrat?

After Knowland swept both primaries in June, I was left with a *fait accompli* in the November General Election. My vote by that time had become meaningless, because my non-partisan registration kept me from participating in the nomination process in the primary. While still considering myself an "independent," I felt it necessary to join one of the political parties in order to make my vote count in the primaries.

Looking at the history of California, I saw that time and again the political advantage lay with Republicans. Cross filing tended to favor the wealthy, who owned much of the mass media, allowing them to spread their message widely and suppress the opposition. Knowland held a terrific advantage right from the start, since his family owned the powerful *Oakland Tribune* and he knew all the major publishers in the state.

An example of media manipulation occurred during the Great Depression. After radical journalist Upton Sinclair won the Democratic nomination and threatened to win the governorship in 1934, Republicans launched a campaign of lies and falsehoods in the media to defeat him. Hollywood produced fictitious newsreels for hundreds of neighborhood theaters that showed shiftless tramps swarming to California on freight cars. On seeing these undesirables on the screen, attracted here by the free handouts promised by Sinclair's radical plan to End Poverty in California (EPIC), voters turned against the

Democrat. But the so-called newsreels that shocked them into voting against Sinclair were fakes!

During the first half of the twentieth century, Democrats held the office of governor only once. That was when Culbert L. Olson was elected in 1938. After one term he was defeated by Earl Warren, who won reelection in 1946 by securing the nomination of three political parties—Republican, Democratic, and Progressive. By means of cross-filing, eight candidates running for statewide office secured victory by becoming the nominees of both parties and twelve others had locked up seats in the House of Representatives the same way.

I wasn't the only one who noticed how cross-filing was weakening the democratic process in California. Someone else who saw the same problem was young idealist Alan Cranston, son of a wealthy San Francisco family, who decided to do something about it. After taking a degree in journalism from Stanford University, he had gone abroad as a foreign correspondent in 1936 for International News Service and saw in person the rise of one-party dictatorships in Europe.

Posted to capitals like Berlin, Germany, Cranston witnessed the Nazi's repression and on returning home two years later, he was shocked to find Americans reading a doctored version of Hitler's *Mien Kampf* which distorted the truth. Having become fluent in German, he was determined to alert the American public. So he translated and published a complete, unadulterated version of Der Fuhrer's diatribe in 1939, which became a best seller. His new, unabridged version revealed all of the venomous and outrageous portions left out of the first translation. Although Cranston was sued for copyright infringement and forbidden to continue publishing his corrected version, he succeeded in getting a half-million copies of the truthful account into the hands of the U.S. public before the case ended.

What I loved about studying political science at Stanford was the give-and-take of graduate seminars and the challenge of reading works by some of the finest minds of all time. Yet I couldn't resist testing the waters of real politics when the chance presented itself in 1952, on learning what Alan Cranston was proposing. A newspaper story told how he sought to balance the scales of political discourse by building a new state voluntary organization to support Democrats in the next election. He was starting a statewide Democratic club movement.

Having decided to register as a Democrat and eager to join the fray, I welcomed the chance to get some grass roots experience. Living at that time in Irvington, a small town in southern Alameda County across the bay from Stanford, I got together with friends and neighbors to organize a local Washington Township club, then got publicity into the newspapers to organize a larger Alameda county group, and finally accumulated enough political clout to choose the officers to run our statewide organization.

The California Democratic Council (CDC) then began exercising its muscle by holding state conventions in Fresno, California, where we passed resolutions and endorsed candidates for upcoming elections. I attended all of them, as a delegate, using my influence to support people and causes in which I believed.

Before long Alan Cranston knew me personally, we met in each other's homes, exchanged ideas on how to win, and while I don't know who was first to suggest it, I urged him to consider running for the U.S. Senate soon after we first met. For years to come, I could count on Cranston to return my phone calls when I needed his advice or assistance. Although our local clubs had very little money, we made up for it with hard work and dedication, passing out handbills, ringing doorbells, and getting stories in newspapers. Soon some of us were getting enough small donations to buy advertising as well.

Our efforts finally paid off in 1958. Democrats swept to power. We won a smashing victory by electing Edmund G. "Pat" Brown to the governorship, took over both houses of the state legislature, and gained every statewide office except secretary of state. The following year cross-filing was abolished by law in California, and four years later Pat Brown was reelected by defeating former presidential contender Richard Nixon for governor.

By this time I'd moved to Santa Clara County, had been appointed to the California Democratic Party State Central Committee, and made dozens of friends in elective office. I also was being urged to run for the California State Senate myself. This was real politics, I knew how to do it, and I loved the opportunities it gave for real accomplishment!

However, I remembered what a seasoned politician had told me years before: "Don't go into politics until you are financially independent, otherwise lobbyists will tempt you with offers you may not be able to refuse." So I accepted a job teaching at San Jose State College which I assumed would take me out of politics. Of course, it didn't, because there are as many politicians in higher education as there are in Sacramento. It soon became clear that you could never escape from politics unless you choose to be a hermit and live in a cave in the Himalayas.

What had I accomplished through all of my volunteer work? Well, I can say without hesitancy, that I helped put a number of good men into public office. In addition to Governor Brown, I helped elect such worthy candidates as Al Alquist, Nick Petris, Carlos Bee, and Robert Crown to the California State Legislature. When I was active in politics, we passed legislation giving California one of the greatest waterways in the world, the California Aqueduct. We also pushed through the California Master Plan for Higher Education as well as laws providing for fair employment practices, consumer rights, and expansive growth of the state economy.

While helping Democrats, one experience proved most memorable. It was meeting and shaking hands with Mrs. Eleanor Roosevelt when she came to Oakland to support those of us working in the California democratic club movement. What I particularly admired about Mrs. Roosevelt was how hard she worked during the Great Depression on behalf of the poor and needy, which is wonderfully detailed in Doris Kearns Goodwin's *No Ordinary Time* and Joseph L Lash's *Eleanor and Franklin.*

In 1958 I was happy to see Alan Cranston elected to the United States Senate, where he served honorably for the next thirty-four years. But after being attacked for questionable campaign fund activities, he chose not to run for a fifth term in 1992 and retired from public life. Although an investigation showed he had violated no law nor any specific rule, the Senate Ethics Committee had charged him with "improper conduct" for accepting huge donations from a savings and loan company, which subsequently went bankrupt and cost the taxpayers millions of dollars. Cranston claimed he was merely representing a constituent and did nothing wrong.

The influence of big money in political financing severely challenges the principle of a government "of the people, by the people, and for the people." Unless we find a way to remove its corrupting influence,

I fear that permitting this practice will destroy our representative form of government. Today lobbyists from K Street in Washington, D.C. continue to ply their trade in the halls of Congress, handing out huge amounts of cash to everyone needing to be reelected and handing it over with the expectation of heavily influencing the way Congress votes on legislation. As one of politics most notorious lobbyists Artie Samish once said, "Money is the mother's milk of politics." The trouble is that today it continues to corrupt both Democrats and Republicans alike, and neither party seems to be either willing or capable of doing anything about it.

There's a happy postscript to all this. While I was heavily engaged on behalf of Democrats, my politically active mother-in-law Mildred Alcock was busy supporting Republicans in Southern California. In her lifelong love of the party of Abraham Lincoln, she was contributing more than ten per cent of her Social Security pension to help defeat Democrats and was put in charge of one of the Republican Party's campaign headquarters in Van Nuys. This former businesswoman was so good at her job that Republican Congressman Joe Holt wanted to recommend her for an appointment as the next Postmistress of Van Nuys. You can't win 'em all!

GOOGLE GUIDE

Chapter 17: I Help Democrats Win

For more on this subject, try these:

"Reagan Campaigns for Truman in 1948." (film). Time: 4:14 min. Find title at YouTube: http://www.youtube.com/

"Will Rogers on Congress." (film). Time: 2:35 min. Find title at YouTube: http://www.youtube.com/

"Is There a Better Way to Choose Our Leader?" by Gordon Greb. (column). http://www.thecolumnists.com/greb/greb8.html/

For a longer listing, go to the book's web site:

Google Brain Book: http://googlebrainbook.blogspot.com/

Chapter 18

Your Big Scoop Can Hurt Us

I wish my life had more "thrill of victory" and less "agony of defeat."

——Mal Hancock (1937-1993)

When the new station manager called, offering me a job at radio station KSJO in San Jose, California, I wondered why he was in Oregon and what he had in mind for me to do. Since the offer had come from old friend Bob Bruce, a talented broadcaster I'd known some years earlier at KVSM in San Mateo, I asked him, "What's going on?"

Bruce said his boss had bought the station and he was coming to California to take charge. The station was a failing operation in a good market, bought by Gordon Allen, owner of a chain of stations in Oregon, and he was sending Bruce to San Jose to make it profitable. It was a real challenge because KSJO was losing twelve thousand dollars a month. "I need to turn this station around in a hurry and I think you can help me do it," Bruce told me. "Come to San Jose and I'll let you have any job there you want."

This employment opportunity came at an opportune moment. I'd completed nearly all of the required course work for the Ph.D. at Stanford, needing only to get ready for language and written examinations before doing the dissertation, which could be done off campus. However, the job situation for my wife Darlene had changed. We were expecting delivery of our first baby in a few months and she would be unable to continue teaching kindergarten.

In addition, my GI Bill entitlements had run out, leaving our savings account very low. To keep going financially, I had tentatively accepted a political appointment at the state capital and was about to leave for Sacramento when this phone call came. It gave me a chance to stay where I belonged, closer to my wife, home, and Stanford.

"Instead of program director," I said to Bruce, "I'd like to set up a first-rate news department at KSJO as a way to show how good local news coverage can build a big radio audience and get you all the sponsors you need. Give me complete control of such an operation as news director and it's a deal."

He answered in the affirmative, the deed was done, and literally overnight I was about to run a radio station like a newspaper. My idea was to turn this small station into the radio equivalent of the *Emporia Gazette* of Kansas, which William Allen White had made into a national powerhouse by giving the community some crackerjack journalism.

At KSJO we subscribed to the radio wire of United Press. Previously I'd learned something about holding wire services to high standards as a graduate student at the University of Minnesota, teaching an undergraduate course in news writing and supervising a daily lab that produced the college's KUOM's "Noon News." As a guest of newspaper editors meeting with the Associated Press's top management at Bemidji, Minnesota, I was amazed seeing these newspapermen severely roasting the AP for being beaten by rival services. They were hopping mad that opposition papers subscribing to the United Press or International News Service had gotten top news stories before the AP and demanded the service do better. They complained bitterly about instances of sloppy reporting, missed stories, or UP beats. That AP Chief got an absolute raking over. But that's the way the AP was kept on its toes all those years.

When I took over as news director of KSJO in San Jose, we were subscribing to the United Press news service. Then in late spring of 1956 several stories started coming off the wire that made me wonder whether there was a bigger story underneath. When I asked United Press Bureau in Sacramento to look into it, Manager Jim Anderson seemed noticeably skeptical, telling me, "Look, Greb, you're in San Jose and this is our territory. The McClatchy news service has five men on the Capitol beat. What could you possibly know 125 miles away that we don't know up here?"

Insisting I knew considerably more about politics than he thought and that it wouldn't hurt to hear me out, he agreed, saying, "Okay! If you think you've spotted something, type it up and send me the facts. I'll need more than guesswork to put a man on it." That's how it began, slowly at first, but before it was over I had helped develop the biggest story to hit United Press news wires "in many a moon" (to quote the exact words of the bureau chief's congratulatory message to me at its end.)

It began simply enough on May 25. That's when the first story appeared that State Treasurer Gus Johnson's son had been forced to resign from a job in his father's office after an audit revealed he had cashed fifty-five bad personal checks. Although young Johnson later made good on each of them, Director of Finance John M. Peirce, whose office spotted the misdeeds, demanded that he be fired. Furthermore Peirce then widened his audit to include all the notes and securities in the Treasury Department, which amounted to several billion dollars. In cash alone, the state treasury had $200 million.

On May 26, State Treasurer Johnson suffered another embarrassment. In this second news story, which originated with the director of finance, a treasury department guard was accused by the state police chief of having deserted his post by crawling out of a window shortly after midnight. That presumably left billions of dollars unguarded on the night of March 4 and required the finance department to send over their own security officers to protect it.

When I spotted both of these United Press stories clattering off the wire into my radio newsroom, coincidentally one after another, I thought something looked strange. Why would the director of finance be the principal source of both news stories, which were embarrassing to a top Republican office-holder? Was something larger at stake?

So I went to the station manager Bob Bruce, saying, "I've got a hunch about those stories coming out of Sacramento. I think something big is in the wind. Mind if I check it out?" Bruce approved my placing long-distance phone calls and running up related expenses. He was as curious about the situation as I was. Soon I began assembling all the data I could find on the situation by placing calls to the principals involved in Sacramento.

By spending every free minute, day and night, reading everything I could find and amassing background material on the major officers involved, I began to put together a theory. What helped was remembering what I'd been taught about banking practices in college. To fulfill an economics requirement, I took a course on "Money and Banking" and learned a few things about the Federal Reserve's role in controlling the flow of money.

Most people pay little attention to the treasurer in any organization as long as he is honest. That's how Californians had long regarded the state treasurer who, as a Republican, had been elected time and again to that office. He was seventy-five years old. On the other hand, I learned that the director of finance was almost unknown, who worked behind the scenes for the governor who appointed him. In truth he was the governor's right hand man and carried out his every wish. Since this made John M. Peirce one of the most powerful men in the Capitol, I now realized he had brought a new name into the picture—Republican Governor Goodwin J. Knight.

On May 30 the deputy assistant treasurer told me that he couldn't talk about the incidents. My questions should be directed to the state treasurer himself. When I placed calls to Gus Johnson at his home and his office, he couldn't be located. By this time I'd been working the phones on Memorial Day, my day off, without too much success. However, I learned that John Pickett, the window-crawling guy, was still working the graveyard shift and I called after midnight to get his side of the story. The guard told me illness had forced him to go to a drugstore for medicine on the night of March 4 and then added angrily, "There's a lot of pressure being put on the state treasurer up here by the director of finance."

That seemed to be an unusual remark. "Pressure? What kind of pressure and why?" On the next day, May 31, Johnson was still unavailable. However, Finance Director Peirce took my call and I got his side of the story. Regarding the guard incident, he said, "That man has been fired." Although I didn't say so, I knew that wasn't true because I'd talked to the guard working at the treasury the night before. Until now I'd refused to reveal my hunch to my associates, saying, "Sorry, I can't tell you what I've got until I know it's true. I wouldn't want to stir up any false rumors."

I now suspected an angry, behind-the-scenes political battle was raging between the governor and the state treasurer. I felt the errant guard had tipped me off when he complained about the state treasurer being under great pressure. But why would one powerful Republican office-holder try to embarrass another powerful Republican unless there was something truly important to gain? What prize was at stake? The bad-check story now had almost died out of the press. With an election coming up on June 5, other stories were taking its place.

On the night of May 31 at home, I had a sudden inspiration. All the pieces of the puzzle began fitting together. So I sat down at the typewriter and composed a brief for Sacramento, suggesting how United Press could help me, saying, "Here are three questions I need answered:

"First, how much state money is deposited in private banks?

"Second, what's the amount in each bank?

"Third, have there been any recent transfers?"

After UP's Wayne Sargent got the assignment and visited the state treasury, he sent me a complete "Cash Accountability Balance Sheet" listing every bank in California where state money was deposited. In a cover letter he wrote, "Does this help you? I have learned that you have been making a number of telephone calls concerning the state's cash. If you have wind of a story, we are here to help you run it down and naturally would see to it that you get the initial scoop. If you have any other questions, sir, shoot 'em along and we'll try our best to get them answered."

I'd suddenly recognized how powerful the state treasurer really was. By determining which banks got California's millions, he could increase or decrease their loaning capability and consequently their profits. The "Fed" on April 13 had raised the "rediscount rate," requiring banks to maintain heavier deposits in order to loan, thereby putting the country into a "tight money" situation. This led me to believe California bankers were eager to get more state money into their vaults and were pressuring their political friends in Sacramento. That's why Knight and Johnson probably were squabbling over where to place these huge state sums!

With this in mind, I asked United Press on June 18 to put a UP man on the story, typed up a five-page summary of my thesis, and said, "In a nutshell, I think that Gus Johnson is being subjected to pressure to operate his department the way someone else wants it run. He resents this. However, he resents it because he is supposed to do something really big. What could this be? Someone up there has to talk to get this out. The Controller won't. The Director of Finance won't. The State Treasurer is the only man who might. He's old. He has had his day. And after what has happened to his son, he may be mad enough to talk. Find out whether he has been asked to move any of the deposits from one bank to another."

The bureau chief assigned Jerry Reynolds to handle the story. He was lucky. He got to see the treasurer, who, in his mid-seventies. was the oldest office-holder in the state. He began asking him about how the treasury was operated and its relationship with other departments of government. Finally Reynolds came to the key question, which he put frankly and boldly, "Has anyone been putting pressure on you to move state money from one bank to another?"

At this, Johnson could restrain himself no longer, replying in anger, "That's been the ever present idea of the governor—" and he unloaded everything he had bottled up. Suddenly the rest of the "big story" began to spill out as the state treasurer unburdened himself. He charged Governor Knight with suggesting he pay off political debts to bankers by depositing huge sums of money in their banks. His accusations confirmed my earlier suspicions and made news headlines, banners, and streamers up and down the state:

TREASURER ACCUSES GOVERNOR

GOVERNOR DENIES CHARGES

INVESTIGATE WHOLE TREASURY

Checking the wire machine at KSJO on June 21, one of my newsroom assistants said, "Hey, Greb. Here's the bulletin you've been waiting for." We hit the airwaves immediately with Johnson's attack on Knight and phoned United Press to extend congratulations. I was given the full interview for exclusive first release over KSJO airwaves before they put it on the wire for clients all over the West.

Within an hour the UP bureau in Los Angeles had the Governor's reaction and the fight was on. San Jose led all other broadcast stations in the state with background, detail, and analysis of what had happened. Hours later every San Francisco Bay Area newscast used it as the lead story as did stations up and down the coast.

When I walked onto the campus at San Jose State the next day, where I'd started teaching radio news earlier in the year, I had a big smile on my face, expecting to be congratulated by everyone in the journalism department for my good work. When I entered the office of Dr. Dwight Bentel, department head, I beamed in proud expectation of getting a hearty handshake.

Have you heard about my big scoop? Yes, he'd read about it that morning in the *San Jose Mercury* but he had no idea of my involvement. It was news to him that an assistant professor of journalism in his own department had been instrumental in bringing to light a big fight between the governor and the state treasurer over state money.

A shadow crossed Bentel's face and he closed the door. Speaking quietly, he told me in hushed tones to keep quiet about what I'd done, "If it ever comes out that you're associated with San Jose State and that the college is involved in this, your big scoop could hurt us. You've got to realize our college budget depends on the good will of Sacramento. We can't afford to offend people up there. For gosh sakes please keep quiet around here about what you've done."

My big story played out for weeks and months thereafter. Gus Johnson fought like a tiger. But the governor, working behind the scenes, finally counter-attacked by having a legislative investigative committee appointed that was stacked with his friends. The committee announced it was calling Johnson before it, would interrogate him thoroughly, and effectively put him on trail. When Johnson learned of this, he had had enough. The state treasurer threw in the towel and resigned.

That explains why I was told to meet with Pat Peabody, wealthy owner of KSJO, to explain why I'd broken this story in the first place. Looking distraught and unhappy when I walked in, it turned out that

Peabody was catching "all kinds of hell at home" about my big scoop from his wife.

"Why would you embarrass Mrs. Peabody this way?" he asked me with a growl. "Didn't you know Gus Johnson was my wife's brother and now she is blaming me for all this bad news coming from my own station?"

I stood before the owner with my mouth open. Holy smokes! I'd dug up facts right and left on this case but never found out about this close family relationship. This could mean I was going to be fired?

But then to my surprise, Peabody rose from his chair, reached across the desk, and shook my hand, saying, "Never mind, Gordon," he smiled. "You were only doing your job. I'll try to deal with this situation at home. But for gosh sakes, please don't let something like this happen again."

And that, ladies and gentleman, explains why I didn't get the Pulitzer prize for breaking the biggest state story of the year. You can't know everything!

GOOGLE GUIDE

Chapter 18: Your Big Scoop Can Hurt Us

For more on this subject, try these:

"Citizen Kane – How to Run a Newspaper." (film). Time: 2:29 min.
http://www.youtube.com/watch?v=tzhb3U2cONs/

"We Take You Now to the United Nations," by Gordon Greb. (script).
http://grebscoop.blogspot.com/

"Do's and Don'ts for Beginning Writers," by Gordon Greb. (article).
http://grebsyndicate.blogspot.com/

For a longer listing, go to the book's web site:

Google Brain Book: http://googlebrainbook.blogspot.com/

Chapter 19

Eureka! I Find the First Broadcaster

Thomas Edison did not invent the first talking machine.
He invented the first one you could shut off.

——Herbert V. Prochnow (1897-1998)

How do you describe the joy of discovery? Is it having a light bulb appear over your head? That's how cartoonists show it. Or is it an emotion that sweeps you off your feet, making you realize what it felt like to be Christopher Columbus, Sir Henry Morton Stanley, or Neil Armstrong.

When it happened to me it was simply jaw-opening astonishment when I realized how important it was. At the same time I also knew that solid evidence needed to be collected right away, published in an academic paper, and told to the world, or it would likely fade away to be forgotten forever. Yet finding this lost history very nearly didn't happen. That I was able to save it was a happy accident. It only happened because I was trying to find someone who had made a significant contribution to journalism.

It began innocently enough. As adviser to a student chapter of the Society of Professional Journalism (Sigma Delta Chi) in 1958, I wanted to honor a major figure in mass communications with a historic marker, particularly someone from San Jose. Since this journalism organization had been founded by newspapermen, most of the honorees had been reporters, editors, or publishers from the print media, such as, Joseph Pulitzer, William Allen White, and H.L. Mencken.

Now I felt it was the turn of someone from the west. What immediately came to mind were outstanding California newspapermen; for example, great San Francisco reporters like Fremont Older, Bret Harte, or Ambrose Bierce. But none of them had worked in the south bay. Wasn't there any notable figure from San Jose? And why not someone from radio which had become part of the press?

A few years earlier, looking for a feature story as news director of a San Jose radio station, I had visited curator Clyde Arbuckle at the city museum and was given a tour of his exhibits. In the course of our tour, Arbuckle stopped for a moment, picked up an odd looking, large black telephone instrument and said matter-of-factly, "This is the original microphone 'Doc' Herrold used when he was running a radio station here in San Jose back in 1909."

Thinking I had not heard him correctly, I asked Arbuckle to repeat what he'd said: "Did I hear you say 1909?" He nodded in assent and I felt something was wrong. History books had long ago settled the question; it was common knowledge that radio began in 1920. As a matter of fact I'd written and produced a radio documentary saluting KDKA as America's first station and aired it in November 1947. Rather than argue, I suggested to Arbuckle that we move along and look at the Donner Party souvenirs and Indian artifacts.

But now in 1958, I remembered Arbuckle's remark and wondered, "Is it possible we actually had a radio station in San Jose long before KDKA?" and decided to check it out. Determined to find the answer, I set off for the college library and at the same time sent a student to see the city historian. When Tony Taravella got back, he gave me his startling news, "Professor, you ought to see what Arbuckle showed me from his files. I think it actually happened in 1909."

What I found in the college library began to give credence to San Jose's claim. There I located two books mentioning the fact that Charles "Doc" Herrold had a radio station in 1909 and was broadcasting regularly by 1912. One of them was in a book on *California* published by the Federal Writer's Project in 1939 and the other, E. P.J. Shurick's 1946 book, *The First Quarter Century of Broadcasting*.

These sources also said the station became KQW after licensing was required in the 1920s. On finding this out and what Arbuckle showed me later from his files, I suddenly realized this was a major find. Eureka!

I may have discovered the world's first broadcasting station. Only I'd have to prove it!

To verify the claim's authenticity I'd need to locate all the original records and present this finding in a scholarly journal. Somewhere, I imagined, there must be a huge trunk filled with Herrold's documents. So I immediately began looking in the phone book to find his family in San Jose. But alas, no luck! No relations turned up. Turning to the next logical source, I called the station itself to let me see its records for use in my article. By now I knew the San Jose operation had been purchased by CBS, its call letters changed to KCBS, and moved to San Francisco.

My first words caught station manager Maurie Webster by surprise. I'd assumed he knew the station's history but he didn't. Webster was astonished on hearing me say, "I'd like to see your files for an article I'm writing for the *Journal of Broadcasting*. Since KCBS is the world's first broadcasting station, I need to let more historians know about it in a scholarly article."

As someone who had been in radio broadcasting since 1932, Webster knew that proving KCBS had predated KDKA by eleven years would revolutionize radio history. He not only pledged full cooperation but also began immediately digging into the station's archives and asking old timers what they knew. "Sure, I always knew we were a pioneer," said Ken Ackerman, a staff announcer since 1941. "I heard Herrold himself talking about it when we put him on the air in a 1945 radio documentary." Then Evelyn Clark, the station's public relations director, phoned me, saying, "We've found something in the files that may help." she said. "When Herrold's first wife visited us several years ago, she told us her last name now is True. She may still be living in your area."

This was a vital piece of information. It almost had me jumping up and down for joy, because it led me to radio schedules, records, photographs, letters, clippings, and people most vital to the Herrold story—Robert True, his 44-year old son and Mrs. Sybil M. True, his 63-year old former wife. When I went to interview them, I found the son had a huge batch of Herrold's records in several cardboard boxes and that his divorced mother had rich memories of the inventor himself. There also was motion picture film showing baby Robert (only a few weeks old in 1914) crying into the microphone while his mother was doing a broadcast.

From the files I found a letter in which Herrold stated, "On January 1, 1909, I opened my School of Radio in San Jose. From the first, broadcasts were a part of my routine... When I opened my school I kept some sort of wireless telephone equipment hooked up all the time." After describing the equipment, he added that "in spite of continual changes in apparatus, there was always music of some sort coming from my station. It was real broadcasting—how do I know? Because I had to make my own audience. I went out through the valley and installed crystal sets so that people could listen to the music."

Herrold's wife Sybil also knew how the San Jose station operated in the old days because she began broadcasting on the station shortly after they were married in 1913. "I really believe I was the first woman to ever broadcast a program," she told me. "I went to Sherman and Clay and arranged to borrow records from them at no cost but just for the sake of advertising the records to these young operators with their little galena sets and we would play these— oh, the up-to-date—young people's records. They would run down the next day to be sure to buy the one they heard on the radio the night before."

She named other pioneers, urged me to find them, and singled out Ray Newby, Herrold's laboratory assistant, as someone who could provide a wealth of information. I found out she was absolutely right. At the age of sixteen, Newby had helped Herrold put the station on the air in 1909 and proved to be a principal eyewitness.

After locating Ray Newby in Stockton, California, I tape recorded him for two hours on my first visit in 1959 and returned to do a sound film interview with him for our college archives in 1978. CBS flew him back to New York City to appear on the program, "I've Got a Secret," on June 29, 1965, where he told a stumped panel and a nationwide audience, "I was the world's first disc jockey."

Recalling for me how it all began, the excitement mounted in Newby as he remembered those first broadcasts: "Yes, when he [Herrold] put this school in operation he had built an umbrella, which spread out over the whole town, practically for a block in every direction ... I think that what started the whole thing—so far as putting the voice out over this large antenna—was when I brought in a little one-inch spark coil and he had a microphone and we connected the thing into a storage battery and talked into this microphone and rattled out some voice. And right away we began to hear telephone calls that they had heard us."

Before it was over I had interviewed dozens of old timers connected to the Herrold station, who confirmed Herrold's early day broadcasting, including:

- Ken Sanders, one of the two young announcers, who were pictured playing music over the Herrold station from an old-fashioned phonograph machine in a 1912 photograph. I interviewed him by amateur "ham" radio in Turlock, California.

- Emil Portal, the other 1912 operator, who although deceased, had left valuable rare and original documents connected to the Herrold station to the Perham electronics museum at New Almaden, California.

- Lee de Forest, early radio inventor, who credited Herrold as the first radio broadcaster when I interviewed him at his North Hollywood home. He remembered picking up Herrold's broadcasts every day at the Panama Pacific Exposition from his radio demonstration booth in 1915.

- Douglas Perham, curator of an electronics museum at New Almaden, California, who not only had one of Herrold's radio transmitters but agreed to put it on display at its original site in downtown San Jose. Perham had heard the San Jose station, while working in Palo Alto in 1912, and told me, "Herrold was broadcasting to audiences regularly when I heard him. Without question he had the first radio station."

Even the most skeptical minds changed. For example, Westinghouse executive Joseph Baudino, representing KDKA, few out to California in 1975 to challenge Herrold's claim. He asked to see all of my records, and having done so, came away convinced that "first station" rights belonged to Herrold. He published this admission in an article he co-authored with Mike Kittross for the *Journal of Broadcasting* in its winter 1977 issue.

What pleased me most, however, after all the time and effort I'd spent looking into the question myself, was what I heard on the radio during the weeklong fiftieth anniversary celebration in 1959. Congratulatory statements were coming from President Dwight D. Eisenhower in the White House, the California Governor and State Legislature, and mayors of major cities. Audiences heard radio stars like Arthur Godfrey in Hawaii, Amos 'n' Andy in Hollywood, and Earl "Fatha" Hines in San Francisco saluting the anniversary; and CBS news correspondents paying tribute to radio's Golden Anniversary from Tokyo, Paris, and London.

I earned not one thin dime from all of this effort but the satisfaction I got from having found an unsung hero of mass communications was reward enough. What better way is there for a teacher to teach?

GOOGLE GUIDE

Chapter 19: Eureka! I Find the First Broadcaster

For more on this subject, try these:

"The Platters 'Remember When' 1959." (song).
Find title at YouTube: http://www.youtube.com/

"The First Lady of Broadcasting," interview by Gordon Greb. (text).
http://grebdiscovery.blogspot.com/

"Charles Herrold, Inventor of Radio Broadcasting," by Gordon Greb and Mike Adams. (book). Find title at Google Books: http://books.google.com/

For a longer listing, go to the book's web site:

Google Brain Book: http://googlebrainbook.blogspot.com/

Chapter 20

War and Peace on Campus

Nothing is real unless it happens on television.

—Daniel J. Boorstin (1914-2004)

When I decided to go on strike at San Jose State College, Governor Ronald Reagan threatened to fire every one of us who dared to take such action. Although Reagan had been, in fact, the former head of the Screen Actors Guild, he had long ago forgotten why workers—teachers as well as actors—had a right to bargain collectively for their wages and working conditions.

Knowing how hard my father's union, the Brotherhood of Fireman and Locomotive Engineers, had fought to obtain these rights made me more determined than ever not to be intimidated by threats of this kind. Thanks to the blessed support of my wife and family, I was able to join about 125 other unionized professors at San Jose State and take a stand for what we believed was right—the right to strike if our employer refused to bargain in good faith over contracts setting forth our salaries and working conditions.

We had been discussing the strike issue at union meetings day and night for weeks and finally put it to a vote just before Christmas. At its height, Local 1362 of the American Federation of Teachers had about 300 members among a faculty of 1200. Reagan had partially succeeded in frightening us with his threat when we struck on January 8, 2009, and we were down to 125 professors when we finally started hitting the picket lines. This is the story of why I was among them.

What I had experienced up to this point teaching at San Jose State College convinced me that the ideals of our founding fathers worked, perhaps not always smoothly and certainly not for everyone right away, but in the long run they did. However, I soon found myself with the responsibility of conducting a professional program in higher education for which there was inadequate funding. With my full budgetary needs ignored, year after year, I was left with no alternative. Collective bargaining seemed to be my last resort.

Finding other faculty as angry and frustrated with their own legitimate needs also unmet, I reasoned that we were left with only two choices: (1) seek employment elsewhere, or (2) try to get these issues solved once and for all. When I could no longer perpetuate this charade, it shocked only those who really didn't know me. Not only did my wife approve my taking a stand but also my staunchly Republican mother-in-law backed me, too, suggesting that she would baby sit our children if my wife had to go back to work after I'd been fired.

I can take credit for having started California's first four-year degree in radio-television news at San Jose State in 1957. We rose to the forefront of journalism education as more of our radio and television students proved themselves on the job and employers began seeking them in greater numbers. The reason was simple. We gave students not only a broad liberal education but practical, hands-on experience in covering news of every kind, dedicated to the highest ethical and professional standards.

It so happened that during most of the 1960s and 70s, my student reporters were covering the protest movement that had American college students protesting across the country. On our campus, they were so busy reporting our college's turmoil, one semester after another that I often felt like the news director of a major station in Washington, D.C. or New York City, lacking only the commensurate budget to cover our needs.

For many months it felt like we had a new crisis nearly every day. Former student David Silverbrand still remembers our slim budget. Now managing KVIQ in Eureka, California, he recently recalled, " ... shooting an entire news story with just fifty feet of 16 mm film was Mr. Greb's weekly ration. It taught me to conserve one hundred per cent and since then I've never seen an out-take that couldn't be used somehow, somewhere."

Our Radio-TV News Center reporters covered everything happening on campus, including protests against recruiting by the Air Force, the Army, the Navy, and the Marines; marches against racial discrimination by the civil rights groups; assemblies to witness draft-card burning; campaigns against the war; ad infinitum. They brought back their stories recorded on 16-mm. film or audiotape, scripted and edited it into news shows to be broadcast over local radio and television stations, and began to take national first place honors in student competitions. What I didn't realize, however, was that someday they would also be recording me on the street carrying a picket sign in support of a strike of professors belonging to the American Federation of Teachers.

San Jose State was noted for doing such a great job that we had no trouble finding stations to put every news program we ever did on the air. One example of this is how we covered the Dow Chemical demonstration. That particular story broke when Students for a Democratic Society objected to a Dow recruiter coming on campus because the company manufactured napalm, a deadly petroleum jelly, which was being used by the Air Force in the Vietnam War. When dropped, this liquid splattered in all directions and too often hit innocent civilians in the target area, clinging to human flesh and burning horribly at more than 2200 degrees Fahrenheit.

A photographer pictured one of its victims in his lens in 1972, which appeared in papers all over the country. It showed a little nine-year old Vietnamese girl, Kim Phuk, crying in pain and running naked down the road after being hit by this weapon. Among the first to recognize napalm's horror and object to its use were Women Against the War in 1966 and then students took it up from coast to coast, the protests finally reaching San Jose State in November 1967.

On the day this confrontation began, College President Robert Clark was away and someone in administration called the city police, fearful of what Students for a Democratic Society were planning to do, as they surrounded the main building on Seventh Street in increasing numbers. Inside a Dow recruiter was waiting for job applicants and outside, growing numbers of students were determined to stop him.

Reporting the scene with a student reporter and film cameraman from a position atop the cafeteria building, I grabbed the microphone, as tensions mounted, to begin describing what was unfolding on campus for San Jose television station, KNTV.

Suddenly a fracas broke out as soon as huge numbers of uniformed cops arrived, formed up, and ordered the students to leave the area. When the crowd failed to disperse, police began marching in formation against spectators and students alike, wearing masks and protective gear, arresting those they could grab and dispelling others by tossing tear gas as they advanced. Although this succeeded in scattering young people in all directions, many crying and gasping for air, it failed to end the protest. Students for a Democratic Society met that night and vowed to return again the next day.

Sensing a bigger news story brewing, KNTV called and offered us a "live feed" from campus the next day, if we could do it. Since our studios already were connected to theirs by cable, Operations Supervisor Glen Pensinger at the Instructional Television Center and Technical Director Bob Reynolds relayed the offer to me.

As the Radio-Television News Center's Executive Producer, I didn't hesitate a minute, telling Pensinger, "If you guys can handle the technical end, my kids can do the rest." The deal was on. I would narrate a "live" feed to KNTV from a TV camera overlooking the scene, switching from time to time to eyewitness accounts from my reporters who would be posted both inside and outside of the college's administration building on Seventh Street.

By airtime, President Clark had returned to the campus and decided to keep uniformed police off campus, devising a new strategy of his own. Standing on a makeshift podium in the middle of the vast crowd, students passed a bullhorn from hand to the hand, debating the issues all afternoon long. Only one instance of overt violence occurred. That was when police arrested several Hells Angels members trying to provoke a fight.

While tensions remained high and arguments reached a fever pitch, it ended peacefully after President Clark came out of the administration building, moved to the center of the crowd, and persuaded the students to go home. He urged them to continue debating the issues elsewhere and then present their grievances to him through student and faculty councils, promising to give their proposals serious consideration.

By the time our news coverage ended, KNTV had preempted three hours of regularly scheduled commercial programming and we assumed our work was over. Then KQED called my office from San Francisco and offered to give us a half-hour that evening on public television if we could handle that. Working feverishly—since we had said yes—Pensinger and Reynolds edited videotape and I did the script, arriving at the station that night, minutes before airtime, and rushing for the control room to inform the director, "Here's the Dow program but I'll need to narrate it live from your announce booth." The next day when dozens on campus asked to see what we'd aired again, they were puzzled by my answer: "Sorry. We can't show the Dow documentary again until it's finished. We haven't yet recorded the narration."

Then came 1968. We watched the nightly news unable to believe what we were seeing. Helplessly we saw our country being torn apart by one tragedy after another—the Rev. Martin Luther King, Jr. cut down by an assassin's bullet in Memphis; four students shot to death by national guardsmen at Kent State; Senator Robert M. Kennedy struck down and killed while campaigning for the presidency in Los Angeles; the Democratic National Convention thrown into confusion by police and protesters rioting outside on the streets of Chicago; and as one breakdown led to another, nobody in authority seemed to know what to do.

When Republicans began looking for a confident, self-assured leader, they found him on horseback in California. Ronald Reagan strode confidently out of the west onto the political stage in 1966 not only with his spurs jingling but also with the scenario voters wanted to hear, promising to put an end to all our troubles. He would crack down on loafers and cheats and take no nonsense from spoiled and arrogant students.

Swept into the governorship on this hard-nosed platform, Reagan kept to his conservative promise and refused to negotiate with dissidents during his entire two terms in office. It became his mantra. He was determined to put "the welfare bums back to work" and "clean up the mess at Berkeley."

What disappointed us was the new role he was playing. Reagan, the former Democrat, union leader, and FDR supporter, had now turned a blind eye to the legitimate poor of our society and the growing opposition to racism and war, which student activists wanted their adult leaders to face. Listening month after month to Reagan's obstinate positions on these issues stirred me to action. These issues were close to my own heart and were being too easily dismissed. When it finally became too much for me to take, I jumped into the fray.

When a combination of frustrations led us to strike at San Jose State in January 1969, I was given the job of handling public relations and getting our story across in the media. This required arranging press conferences, mailing publicity, taking telephone calls, and being interviewed for radio and television. Although I worked closely with Local 1362 leaders and tried to coordinate our efforts, it was difficult with so many varied interests involved. With every Tom, Dick, and Harry trying to get into the press, what I finally accomplished under these adverse circumstances was really amazing.

We established strike headquarters close to campus in a house owned by Dr. John Sperling, statewide AFT leader and local union officer. I became the chief spokesman for the views of our union and those of Dr. Eldred "Al" Rutherford, Local 1362 President. During the day, I took phone calls from wire services, networks, and reporters everywhere, responding as best I could to the onslaught coming from all sides—the governor, trustees, politicians, and colleagues on campus who disagreed with our stand—by holding regular press conferences. Each night we held union meetings to discuss and vote on the issues.

With Reagan lambasting us day after day from Sacramento, I had to figure out ways to counteract his exaggerated claims and get more people on our side. Then an opportunity for me to invade the lion's den dropped into my lap. It happened the day he picked on San Jose State College at a press conference, placing blame for the campus disorder squarely on the shoulders of Dr. Al Rutherford, head of our union, and promising that Rutherford would be the first professor fired when it was all over.

This attack was so mean spirited it drove me to take action. I grabbed a phone and placed a call to John Vasconcellos, our Democratic assemblyman from San Jose, luckily got him on the line, and argued for our right to reply. "It's not fair to let Reagan smear people without a chance of answering," I pleaded. "I think Rutherford should answer these accusations in Sacramento itself if you can find a place for him to do it." Vasconcellos agreed and got us the best place possible—the same room at the capitol as the one used by the governor when he made his accusations. Now Rutherford would meet the Sacramento press corps on Reagan's own turf.

Speaking directly to the question of why we were striking, AFT union head Al Rutherford accused Governor Reagan of neglecting state college needs, wanting to deny us our right to peaceably assemble, and refusing every petition to redress the grievances. Al stood at the podium like a seasoned politician, taking questions from left and right, and scoring on one point after another. We were overjoyed at the play this news story got afterward. We heard Rutherford's statements leading every radio station's five-minute newscast as we were driving home. It was the top story at 2 o'clock and again at 3 o'clock. Then at 4 o'clock it was gone.

Taking its place was drug culture weirdo Timothy O'Leary, speaking on behalf of the strike at San Jose State and urging everybody to "turn on, tune in, and drop out." Some idiot had brought O'Leary to our campus that afternoon and effectively killed the Rutherford story.

When the strike ended, it was through negotiation. College administrators and members of the academic council didn't want us fired. Nor did many influential politicians in Sacramento. The outcome reminded me of what one student told me before the strike began, "If they fire everyone who went on strike, we're going to lose the best teachers in the college."

San Jose State College President Robert Clark wasn't happy with Reagan's policy and he wanted all of his professors back. He proposed that if we agreed to settle the strike and the state insisted on firing us, he would immediately rehire us at the same rank, position, and pay level as before. We would, however, have our salaries docked for every day we had been absent. When the list of 63 professors being penalized was published in the *San Jose Mercury*, mine led the list.

After the dust had settled, it appeared that we'd lost every one of our demands. But Dick Meister, labor reporter for the *San Francisco Chronicle* saw it differently, concluding that the strike "showed that teachers can strike, despite the existence of laws against public employee strikes … It showed that teachers unions can negotiate for its members … It helped push much larger and more powerful teacher organizations into demanding what amount to union rights."

All 125 strikers, except one, got their jobs back. A new governor and state legislature approved collective bargaining for teachers a few years later. By that time some of those who had been strikers had become chairmen, deans, and leaders of the state academic council, and assistants to the chancellor. I was by this time head of the Graduate Program in Mass Communications.

Professor John Sperling, Ph.D., who was state chairman of the American Federation of Teachers during the strike, returned to teaching at San Jose State but quit public education a few years later to start his own highly profitable private educational institution, the University of Phoenix. Today he is a successful billionaire.

Professor Al Rutherford, Ph.D., head of AFT Local 1362, who was the only one of us singled out for firing, spent years in court fighting his dismissal and after finally winning his case, quit the state of California, moved to Oregon, and died there some years later in obscurity.

Ronald Reagan, with a grin on his face and a wave of his hat, moved to Washington, D.C. and never had to make a "B" movie in Hollywood ever again.

GOOGLE GUIDE

Chapter 20: War and Peace on Campus

For more on this subject, try these:

"The Beatles – Here Comes the Sun." (song).
Find title at YouTube: http://www.youtube.com/

"Ronald Reagan Versus The Hippies." (television) Time: 2:00 min.
Find title at YouTube: http://www.youtube.com/

"You and Public Relations," by Gordon Greb. (text).
http://grebtv.blogspot.com/

For a longer listing, go to the book's web site:
Google Brain Book: http://googlebrainbook.blogspot.com/

Chapter 21

American Imbecile in France

What I got by going to Canada was a cold.

——Henry David Thoreau (1817-1862)

If you hand me a book, magazine, or newspaper containing strange words, what they look like on paper hold no particular fascination for me. But if I hear those same words spoken to me in a foreign tongue, they no longer are alien sounds but come alive as beautiful music. The significance of this fact took me a long time to recognize.

My earliest effort to unravel this jungle of foreign communication and understanding began in the seventh grade. The brave teacher who tried to guide me through the labyrinth of the Spanish language was dark-haired, tall, and soft-spoken Miss Hall. She placed me in the first row to keep an eye on me and since I was somewhat taken by her attractive appearance, I tried to reciprocate by just looking at her and thinking how beautiful she was.

Because someone told me that this lovely senorita was related to the famous co-author of *Mutiny on the Bounty*, James Norman Hall, I made a valiant effort to please her. But it was of no use. While Miss Hall tried patiently to jam bits and pieces of *espanol* into my thick head, very little of it stuck.

Questioning me one day as to why I wasn't studying, I was surprised to hear a schoolmate speak up in class and volunteer in my defense, saying, "Oh, I've seen Gordy walking home with his Spanish book every afternoon." That was true. But I never opened it or spent a minute reading it. It was too boring for a red-blooded American boy with other, more exciting things to do. Despite my laziness and chosen incompetence, I'm still indebted to Miss Hall for what she must have seen in me in the end. She gave me a passing grade. For that I say, muchas gracias for being a true friend of a young and struggling student, knowing that someday I'd wake up and settle down.

Sorry to say, English bothered me from the start, too. Some kind of dyslexia plagued me from childhood. Learning simple ABCs troubled me from the moment I graduated from kindergarten. While I loved reading at an early age, I had trouble distinguishing between the letters "m" and "n." An old photograph proves this was a problem. It shows me as a teenager, standing bare-chested, and arms folded alongside my twelve-year old chum Jack Corbett atop a mound of earth in his backyard.

The picture celebrates the fact we'd done something adventuresome. We had succeeded in becoming Neanderthal men who lived in a cave. That summer with picks and shovels we spent our afternoons digging a deep pit in Jack's backyard, which we turned into a cave by laying wooden boards over the gaping hole, covering the planks with earth, and fashioning a long trench, using the same engineering devices to create our secret entrance.

To get into the main chamber you had to crawl on hands and knees through a long, dark, underground tunnel and then close the swinging door behind you by pulling on a rope. Inside we'd light candles and sit in the semidarkness giggling over the fact nobody knew where we were. When we came out we were so proud of this accomplishment, we got Jack's mother to snap a photo of us with her Kodak camera, picturing two boys, arm in arm, holding a sign that read, "CAVE MEM OF 1934". Guess who printed the sign?

My supreme test—the Super Bowl of Foreign Language Learning—finally came in college. From the moment I walked through Sather Gate wearing a Blue and Gold freshman beanie at UC Berkeley, I began wrestling with two foreign languages, Spanish and French. They were needed to satisfy the university's undergraduate requirements. Thus began my long struggle with foreign languages that challenged me all the way through graduate school.

As a Ph.D. candidate I remained confounded by the need to acquire a reading knowledge of German and French. Seated at my desk one day, pouring over *Shorter German Reading Grammar,* the language book my German instructor F. W. Strothmann had assigned me, I studied every word as carefully as a prisoner locked up in Alcatraz hoping to find a way to escape. Recognizing that in Old German each word beginning with an "f" should be treated as the equivalent of a modern "s" was the first obstacle to be faced. Then figuring out what should be the proper placement of the verb in each German sentence became the challenge.

Too often my translation turned out to read, "Throw the cow over the fence some hay." But I plugged along in what seemed a hopeless and vain effort to crack the code and decipher each word, sentence, and paragraph correctly. Then, at the start of one of the chapters, words of advice in English suddenly grabbed my full attention when the sentence said, "Learn the following verb forms by heart." Instantly my brain did a complete somersault and began translating the idiom from Old English into American English.

What those words said to me now was, "Don't hate your work but love what you're doing." No wonder Italian, French and Spanish could be called the Romance Languages. Linguists trace the term to its Latin origins but I know now that isn't the real reason. It's that love makes the world go round.

So I began courting French by taking an imaginary trip to Paris. By picking up posters, newspapers, and magazines from a travel agency, I turned my study into a miniature Parisian cafe. To give it as much authenticity as possible, I began searching for a way to bring the sights and sounds of France into my life through radio. With the help of a cheap, second-hand, Japanese short-wave receiver, I began searching the wireless spectrum for foreign programs. I picked up Spanish language programs easily from Central and South America on my roof antenna, but my little radio couldn't quite reach Paris. What I did get, however, were French programs from the *Voice of America, Radio Canada,* and *Radio Cuba* (that aimed its propaganda at French Canadians).

To supplement what radio provided, I went bargain hunting for *Moulin Rouge* albums, building a library of chansons by such vocalists as Jacqueline Francois, Edith Piaf, Henri Decker, and Juliette Greco. When they became available, I bought complete albums in Spanish,

German, Italian, Japanese and French. What a pleasure it was to dream of sitting at a sidewalk table alongside the Champs-Elysees, sipping a bit of wine while doing my homework, as Edith Piaf sang a sad song.

Was it the voice of this lovely chanteuse singing mournful lyrics that did it? Or was it my atmospheric Left Bank room whose walls were covered with gorgeous posters of the Eiffel Tower, Montmartre, and Arc de Triomphe? Voila! When this environmental setting enabled me to conquer French, I used the same ideas to tackle German, turning my study into a Munich beer hall at Oktoberfest. I'm amazed at how easily people from foreign lands learn our language. Yet the trick must be the same for all. It's what the French say about women, "Vive la difference!"

When you immerse deeply into something and welcome different sounds and sights into your life, you'll soon start to "get it." It's what strangers do when they come to our country. Shopping one time in a San Jose department store and noticing that the young sales woman spoke to me with a German accent, I politely asked her to tell me how she learned English.

"Oh, I knew very little English when I first came to America," she said. "But then I began watching television every day and by paying attention to what people were saying in the commercials I began learning. Simple idea, don't you think? *Nicht whar?*"

My success emboldened me to begin thinking big. By learning to love foreign languages, I not only passed my exams in German and French but also brought about this accomplishment by taking an imaginary trip to Europe. It's no wonder that my wife, Darlene and I then decided to visit the lands where these languages actually were spoken.

The Golden Gate International Exhibition in 1939 had whetted my interest in other cultures and nations by offering small versions of themselves to visitors. Exhibit books advertised: "Be our guests at Cafe Brazil, where you may sip Brazilian coffee amid restful tropical surroundings." Nations from around the world opened the eyes of Americans to the delights of Australia, China, Dutch East Indies, El Salvador, France, Guatemala, Indochina, Italy, Japan, New Zealand, and Norway.

Twenty years later we elected to fly to Europe on a propeller driven DC 7B, which began an odyssey that's never stopped. Our first challenge was to understand the French—the people—not necessarily the language. In France we were given the raspberry from the moment we landed at Orly airfield and got into a taxi bound for the Opera Quarter of Paris. From the moment we stepped into a cab, the driver seemed extremely unruly.

When we told him to take us to "The hotel of the United States," his response was a grunt. Then he made a sour face, pursed his lips, and gave out a loud raspberry. Thinking he misunderstood my words, I repeated them slowly and got the same unflattering insult. He took off, gave us a wild and bumpy ride, and finally stopped at the hotel. He turned around and held out his hand for payment. The meter said one thing and the cabbie another. When I counted out the correct number of French francs, he shook his head and held up his fingers demanding more.

Darlene whispered, "Don't argue." So I paid what he asked, feeling glad he hadn't driven off with our luggage. At the desk, we got another disappointment. The clerk ignored the fact our travel agent had made reservations and directed us to a much smaller abode a few blocks down the street. Thus it went. Rude service, unfriendly receptions, and signs on walls: "Yankees, Go Home."

No wonder a few days later we gladly said farewell and took our next plane to Zurich, Switzerland. Nowhere in Paris on this five-day visit did we find a "welcome mat" out for visiting Americans. Because we experienced much of the same on repeated visits to Paris, we vowed never to return to that unfriendly city ever again. What broke our resolve and changed our minds was that some friends wanted us to visit them in Spain a few years later. Since the cheapest way to get there would be to take a coach tour out of London, we chose an itinerary taking us by ferry across the English channel, through several old cities in France we hadn't seen before, and delivering us for a week at a Mediterranean holiday hotel near where they lived in Spain. The only glitch was we had to return by way of Paris. The price being right, we decided to grin and bear it.

Our Thompson company tour guide, who met us inside Victoria railway station in London early in the morning, directed us to the passenger car. As we settled into the British Rail car for our journey to Dover, we noticed we were the only Americans in the group. Everyone else seemed British and knowledgeable about what to do next. Friendly old English ladies were opening little containers for sandwiches and drink, while their husbands sank comfortably in their seats to enjoy a newspaper, *The Times, Guardian,* or *Sun.* We had to be content to look out the window at cows in the meadow, distant trees on a hill, and lofty clouds in the sky.

When our train arrived, there was more hurly burly. The British already were out the door first with their suitcases, bags, and goods in hand, and they were all running as fast as they could toward the passenger ferry, sitting at the dock. By the time we found the proper deck, all the good seats had been taken by quick-witted Brits who knew the routine. Others, who had someone saving their seats, were already standing in line at the canteen to buy more food and drink. And with everyone rushing around and the loudspeaker barking away, the ship lifted anchor and loud noise of the motors told that we were under way.

Approaching Calais and wanting to be among the first to disembark, my wife and I made an early move and were happily leading those going ashore. Hurrying down the ramp to the long corridor leading to the Customs Office, I caught sight in the distance of two overhead signs which read in English: "Visitors With Landing Cards, Go Right" and "All Others, Go Left."

"Hey! What's this?" I asked one of the English matrons briskly walking along with me. "I don't have a Landing Card. Where did you get it?"

"Oh, too bad for you and too late now," she sniffed knowingly. "You were supposed to get that card aboard ship. Didn't you hear the announcement on the public address system?"

Now coming to the division point, Darlene and I dreaded turning left and facing our doom. We felt stupid, helpless, and utterly embarrassed. Off to our right were our English companions with their proper credentials moving swiftly along and here were we, two ignorant Yanks, going to the left and straight into the arms of the French authorities. Ahead we could see through the window that one poor man already was being interrogated by a tall uniformed customs officer and hanging his head in shame. *Mon Dieu*!

Now the French were going to give me the raspberry one more time! Humiliated beyond belief, I walked sheepishly up to the surly looking, dark-suited gendarme, knowing in my imagination he was going to say: "No one is admitted to La Belle France without proper authorization. Where is your official Landing Card, Mr. Yankee Doodle? Why don't you have one?"

Pulling myself together and collecting all the dignity a condemned man can possess, I looked this stern man in the eye and confessed that neither I nor my dear wife had in our possession the required Landing Card, saying, "*Je suis un American imbecile*" (which was a close as I could come to confess that I was a completely stupid American). This French guard looked stunned. His expression slowly changed, took on a face of someone surprised, and then he broke into a wide grin. Addressing me in perfect English, he said, "Don't worry, madam and monsieur. Your passport and your honesty are enough. Your papers are in order! Welcome to France!"

Darlene and I picked up our luggage and glanced back to see all the British tourists jammed up before the right hand entrance, stretched out in a long line. By attempting to speak to the customs officer in his own language—even though it was my own "fractured French"—I, the dumb Yankee, got into France first. From that time forward—no matter how little we knew of the language—my wife and I have decided to speak the tongue of every country we would visit in the future. When we tried it again on our next trip to Paris, people laughed, became friendly, and welcomed us to their country. The dumb thing is never to try.

GOOGLE GUIDE

Chapter 21: American Imbecile in France

For more on this subject, try these:

"How to Speak French." (film). Time: 3:52 min.
Find title at YouTube: http://www.youtube.com/

"Metropole Paris email from Gordon Greb: Paris: It's for Old Lovers, Too." http://www.metropoleparis.com/1998/304/email304.html/

"Dover Ferry Crossing to Calais, France." (film). Time: 2:11 min.
Find title at YouTube: http://www.youtube.com/

For a longer listing, go to the book's web site:

Google Brain Book: http://googlebrainbook.blogspot.com/

Chapter 22

Lost in China: Help, Marco Polo!

*A foreign correspondent is someone who flies around
from hotel to hotel and thinks the most interesting thing
about the story is the fact that he has arrived to cover it.*

——Tom Stoppard (1937-)

We got off the train at 3:30 in the morning and stepped onto the platform of a railway station in the black of night. Not a single light was showing. With nobody there to guide us, we had to carefully make our way over the bodies of sleeping Chinese in search of an official tour guide, who simply wasn't there.

It didn't take long to realize we were forgotten tourists in a dire predicament. There was nobody at the station to meet us, and nobody in our small group of four people spoke more than two words of Chinese ("knee how" for hello and "she she" for thank you). This was the situation facing my wife Darlene and me one early morning in late spring of 1985. We were lost somewhere in the middle of the People's Republic of China because our tour agency had let us slip through the cracks.

Everything went well at first, arriving in Shanghai by plane, being met by a uniformed English-speaking guide at the airport, and seeing China by train for the first part of our tour of the ancient capitals of China. We soon become accustomed to being met in one city after another by English-speaking guides. That is, until, without warning, we found ourselves, on this dark and cold morning, abandoned in a railroad station somewhere in the middle of China, not knowing where to turn to next.

The Chinese tour operator in Hong Kong had flown us to Shanghai the week before without a tour guide because our group was exceedingly small. We were only four people, a number so minuscule that an American company probably would have canceled the trip. But the Chinese were so anxious to earn dollars that they arranged a tour for us anyway—two Americans and two Australians—our companions being Dave and Carolyn, a young couple on holiday who wanted to experience China on their honeymoon.

When it finally dawned on us that nobody was there to meet us, someone said, "Let's find the lounge for soft seaters," the category used by the Chinese for tourists traveling First Class. Though it was after three o'clock in the morning, we pounded on the door and awakened the attendant, a dour old Chinese woman, who, half-asleep, let us inside. Obviously she wanted to do whatever it took to quiet us down, then get back to sleep.

Motioning for us to wait, she disappeared out the back door. We collapsed on comfortable lounges ("soft seats"), somewhat happy and grinning from ear to ear in the mistaken belief we were being rescued. In five minutes we were disabused of that assumption. The elderly attendant came back and motioned us outside to a standing taxi and, with a few words in Chinese to its driver, shoved us inside and sent us on our way.

We had no idea where the taxi was taking us. However, during the ride we had amazing sights. In the early light of dawn we could make out hundreds of Chinese in the open, doing all sorts of curious contortions with their arms, legs, and bodies, which we later learned were Tai Chi exercises, an ancient art good for both body and soul. Again we believed we'd been rescued when the taxi driver dropped us off in front of a "western style hotel." We paid him a small sum, went inside, and rushed to the front desk to be "rediscovered."

Ah, yes, the clerk smiled in English, he would "check the records." After a short time, he came back with the discouraging news: "No, the hotel has never heard of you." There was no record of us and nobody there would accept responsibility. Could anyone here help? "No, you come here on your own—go away on your own," they more or less told us.

By this time young David's temper was rising and he said firmly, "We're going to phone the tour headquarters at the next city—Xian— and demand that the Chinese tour operator do something about this." Luckily telephones were available upstairs at the hotel, so David and I climbed the stairs to make long-distance phone calls while the women waited in the lobby. After more than an hour of trying, we had no luck reaching anybody in Xian.

Downstairs, our wives had the bright idea of saying, "Hello, do you speak English" to every Chinese person who walked through the lobby. We returned to discover that Darlene and Carolyn had found a friend. They were talking animatedly with an old Chinese gentleman. He spoke excellent English. He had learned it fifty years earlier in a school run by missionaries in the 1930s. "Yes," he said. "I will help you, but first I need approval from my boss."

In a communist-run state, individual initiative wasn't encouraged and authority needed to be consulted. So I accompanied the kindly old gentleman upstairs to meet his boss. He handed me his card and I learned that our new Chinese friend was a design engineer. He introduced me to his boss, got permission to help me, and we returned downstairs.

Thank goodness, I thought to myself, we've found a kind soul to lead us out of this wilderness. In the lobby we talked things over and decided to take the train to Xian. Our Chinese gentleman arranged for a taxi to the station, went with us to buy the train tickets, and helped us aboard when it arrived. Ah, what luck! Our Chinese friend spoke to the conductor and got a four-person compartment for our next overnight journey.

Before leaving, I rummaged through my suitcase, found a blank envelope, and handed him my pen, saying, "Please write down your name and address so that I can send you our thanks." He did and returned the envelope just as we began pulling out.

So I leaned out the window, fairly shouting, "What can I send you from America?" He shouted back, "Stamps! I am a stamp collector." As our train slowly moved away, I looked back to see our rescuer slowly disappear, a lone figure waving till we were out of sight. Were we saved? Not quite! But now we were experienced innovators.

On board I heard English being spoken by a passenger in one of the compartments and introduced myself to a young Swedish girl who was in China as a student in Beijing. She was fluent in Chinese as well as English, and was escorting her mother and a friend to Xian. After learning of our plight, she took us on as a volunteer tour guide and we followed her aboard a bus in Xian, riding till we reached a Russian-style hotel, where we all got off, dumped our luggage, and tried to secure a room.

By this time we were getting desperate. To stay there, we had to guarantee the Chinese hotel that if we were given a room and all our meals, we agreed to pay if the tourist office didn't. By this time young David's temper was red hot and he marched into the tourist office the next morning, refusing to leave until somebody took responsibility. This got immediate attention. But it also left the Chinese somewhat bewildered by having a young Australian staging a one-man sit-down strike in a communist country.

It took nearly eight hours more to untangle this bureaucratic mess. Finally the mistake was realized after somebody made the right phone calls and discovered our names on a list. Hurrah! The truth of our situation became apparent and the Chinese shamefacedly admitted, "Yes, you are on our list. But you came to Xian too soon. Why did you leave the previous city early?"

Our reply was "Sorry, there was nobody there to greet us, we were stranded and had to come." I don't know whether the Chinese have an expression like "somebody goofed," but once they recognized their mistake they couldn't have been more apologetic. Once we were officially recognized as their tourists, we were treated like royalty—taken to the finest restaurants, to see Chinese opera, visit Xian museums, and drive by private van to exotic and interesting places most tourists never have time to see. We could do all these things because we had extra days. We were accorded every privilege they could think of to make amends for their error.

How Marco Polo got around China using the Italian language I'll never know, but we four "innocents abroad" managed fairly well using only a couple of textbook expressions and meeting friendly people fluent in both English and Chinese. Today I still use "knee how" and "she she" in Chinese restaurants and get an appreciative smile and what seems like first class service by their polite demeanor! Oh, yes, our friend, the English-speaking Chinese gentleman, did get his packet of stamps! You bet, in a big envelope with a card saying THANK YOU in capital letters. That was many months after we finally got home to California from our adventurous six-month trip around the world.

GOOGLE GUIDE

Chapter 22: Lost in China: Help, Marco Polo!

For more on this subject, try these:

"Learn Chinese – Speak Chinese – My name is and I am from." (film). Time: 2:12 min. Find title at YouTube: http://www.youtube. com/

"President Nixon goes to China – Part 17 of 28." (film). Time: 4:54 min. Find title at YouTube: http://www.youtube.com/

"Learn Chinese with NBC's Show Al Roker at WLE China Study abroad Beijing campus." (NBC film). Time: 5:48 min. Find title at YouTube: http://www.youtube.com/

For a longer listing, go to the book's web site:

Google Brain Book: http://googlebrainbook.blogspot.com/

PART III

THE SUPER EGO

If there is a purpose in life at all, there must be a purpose in suffering and dying. But no man can tell another what this purpose is. Each must find out for himself and must accept the responsibility that his answer prescribes.

——Gordon W. Allport (1897-1967)

Chapter 23

A Philosopher Learns to Laugh

Forgive, O Lord, my little jokes on Thee
And I'll forgive Thy great big one on me.

——Robert Frost (1874-1963)

One night at a party I overheard someone say, "Why are we here?" I turned to see that it was Major George Dewey, husband of an office secretary at San Jose State College. He was a middle aged, retired U.S. Army officer, talking to other guests, and I could see he had a serious look on his face.

Both his wife and I worked for the publications manager of the college, Lowell Pratt, who with his spouse was hosting the party. Having overheard the question, Mr. Pratt turned to the major with a smile, saying, "I thought you knew. You're here because it's our wedding anniversary."

Those of us standing around, enjoying light cocktails, looked at the major, who obviously was deep into his cups. He flung his hand in the air and said, in quiet desperation, "No, you don't understand. What's our purpose on this earth? Haven't you ever thought about that?"

But before anyone could answer, Mrs. Pratt emerged from the kitchen, hurrying to the table with a huge, steaming platter of food, and she invited us to be seated for dinner. The question was left hanging in the air—unanswered—and soon everybody forgot about it.

Fortunately it's a question philosophers have been asking for ages. We can go back, for example, to thousands of years ago when various wise men discussed the meaning of life at another party, their answers written down and saved for our elucidation today. It happened in the fourth century B.C. among a party of Greeks, laughing and arguing as they walked from Piraeus, the port of Athens, to their homes in the city. They, too, went to festivals on more than one occasion and were connoisseurs of wine. Wine, it seems, cultivated the mind. And on this particular night they paid keen attention to every word spoken by Socrates, as Plato was copying down what he was saying about the great questions of life.

If you haven't yet read Plato's "Allegory of the Cave" in his *Republic*, and his other musing on truth and knowledge, you'd be wise to do so, preferably while seated comfortably under a tree, isolated, and undisturbed, since peace and quiet favors understanding of such great books and great minds. But wisdom isn't a monopoly of the ancients. We've had them in the twentieth century, too, and I'm audacious enough to break with scholarly tradition and suggest that you'll find some of the answers to Major Paul's question in a Hollywood movie.

There's something more than screen entertainment in the acclaimed 1948 film *The Treasure of Sierra Madre*, the work of the mysterious writer B. Traven and the director John Houston, whose film focuses on the hungers, ambitions, suffering, jealousies, and dreams of ordinary human beings. What the picture gives us is a close-up look at the struggle of three desperate men, who in striving for a better future, find that they must overcome numerous dangers to fulfill their needs and aspirations, and just when they think they've achieved success, things don't work out as planned. When their quest for treasure ends in failure and the survivors are faced with a dark and empty future, they have to ask themselves, "Was it worth it? What are we left with now?"

The story of *The Treasure of Sierra Madre* begins with two Americans—Fred C. Dobbs (Humphrey Bogart) and Bob Curtin (Tim Holt)—down and out in Mexico in the 1930s when they encounter a grizzled old gold prospector, Howard (Walter Huston), in a flophouse. Finding themselves broke and hungry, they become convinced he knows how to find the precious metal, and using Dobbs's lottery winnings, they equip themselves and set out for the rugged Sierra Madre.

However, the two inexperienced members of the party, unaccustomed to living in the wilds, are quickly worn down. They start grumbling with disappointment after weeks of stumbling up and down mountains and valleys. Tired and weary at this useless searching, the young men are ready to quit. Then old Howard jumps up and begins dancing a jig. "You're too dumb," he laughs. "You wouldn't know gold if you saw it." With obvious glee, he tells them they've found the mother lode.

Elated by their discovery, the trio sweat and toil to dig out its riches, divide it up, and after months of labor, load their bags of wealth onto pack animals and start back to civilization. Then Dobbs, slowly going insane, starts mumbling to himself because he suspects the others are planning to steal all the gold. In his paranoia, he attacks Curtin, leaves him for dead, and heads down the mountainside alone, pushing and cursing the burros.

Now completely out of his mind, he is no match for banditos, who kill him, toss the sacks aside, and steal the burros. When Howard finds Curtin and the two arrive at the Mexican village, they learn that Dobbs had made their joint enterprise a complete disaster. They're broke once again and faced with the question, "What do we do now?"

Realizing that Dobbs' insanity had caused their sacks of gold to be stolen, torn open, and blown away, Howard teaches young Curtin, his only surviving partner, that they can still go on. The older man explains to his surviving partner that they should simply take stock of their current situation and make new plans for the future. The old man thinks over what's happened, tells his partner they should appreciate they've come out alive, and then breaks out into a grin. "Laugh, my boy," he says. "It's Nature's joke, because the gold has blown back to the mountain."

This reminds me of the positive attitude my father had during the Great Depression. Faced with the need to support a family and lacking a steady job, he seldom, if ever, showed any outward signs of insecurity, anger, or emotion over his obvious frustration at not finding a steady job. He simply got up each morning, put on his suit and tie, and took whatever work was offered. While not overtly a religious man, he never seemed discouraged and bitter but always wished for a better tomorrow and carried on.

As long as we had enough for food and clothing, a house over our head, and an extra dollar or two, Pop always found moments when he could laugh. My mother, brother, and I could hear him laughing in the other room whenever he sat down to read the newspaper, because he never skipped the funnies and always turned to the *Katzenjammer Kids* and *The Gumps* with bursts of glee. It's also why my father took us to see lots of movies with Buster Keaton, Charlie Chaplin, and Laurel and Hardy. Their mishaps and troubles helped us all keep our own spirits up.

Laughter always filled our house. One time Pop walked into the kitchen with a puzzled look on his face and said to my mother, "Irene, just a minute ago I was thinking of something and now I can't remember what it was."

Mom, being busy at the stove, barely turned her head, and mumbled a reply, "That's no problem," she said. "You'll remember if you go 'vacuum the room'."

"What?" Pop answered. "Why would vacuuming the room restore my memory?"

"I'm sorry," Mom said with a big smile on her face. "I didn't mean to get out the vacuum clearer. What I meant to say was you should 'go back to the room' and then that thought will come back to you."

They both broke out laughing. It was a ridiculous misunderstanding and it became one of the jokes they shared together for the rest of their lives. There's no question that this positive attitude influenced me in choosing my own partner for life, because I had no trouble proposing marriage when I found a young woman who exhibited many of these same qualities.

Obviously Darlene was lovely to look at. But so were many other girls I had dated, but none of them was quite like this little kindergarten teacher whom I met on a blind date. We seemed to easily enjoy each other's company and what was more important, she laughed at my jokes. She exhibited such a good-natured spirit and happy outlook on life you couldn't help feeling elated in her presence. That's because she truly was happy.

If Darlene saw something special in me, she didn't tell me at the time, but she did tell her mother, who drove from Van Nuys to San Bernardino to look me over. What neither of them knew, however, was that my mother had told me how to find the right girl. She said, "Gordon, to know how the girl will turn out, study the mother."

That settled it. That summer on my way back to the University of Minnesota to submit my thesis and complete my master's degree, I'd stopped off at Eugene, Oregon, to accept an offer to teach at the university there in the fall and had to decide what to do next. So I on arriving in Minneapolis, I composed the most important piece of writing of my life. I air mailed a marriage proposal to Darlene who was vacationing with her mother at Honolulu, Hawaii.

Fortunately for me, she accepted. And why not? She was there with her mother—a vibrant, cheerful, outgoing, and competent businesswoman with whom I got along fabulously. Years later, when Darlene found out my emphasis on the appealing features of her mother had influenced my marriage proposal, I found it nearly impossible to criticize her personally about anything thereafter. She would always respond, "If that's what you wanted, you should have married my mother."

On a recent visit to Dr. Julie Archer, our family physician, she recommended a book for me to read after I told her how laughter had gotten me through many adversities in life and hoped it would help in the future. "But realistically," I said, "I guess a smile can't be my umbrella all the time. I often think of those poor victims of the Nazi prison camp who had nothing to laugh about." At this Dr. Archer smiled, saying, "I think you should read Viktor Frankl's *Man's Search for Meaning*," and added, "I believe there's something in there for you." She was right.

Viktor Frankl was a Jewish psychiatrist who survived three years in those terrible concentration camps. He remembered the smile of his wife was what helped him endure endless days of misery. In describing those horrible conditions in his 1945 book, he wrote, "… an outsider may be even more astonished to hear that one could find a sense of humor there as well; of course, only the faint trace of one, and then only for a few seconds or minutes. Humor was another of the soul's weapons in the fight for self-preservation."

Roman Gary, who escaped the Holocaust and authored *The Roots of Heaven*, concluded that humor "is an affirmation of dignity, a declaration of man's superiority to all that befalls him."

Victor Hugo, nineteenth century author and human rights activist, who wrote *Les Miserables*, considered laughter to be "the sun that drives winter from the human face."

Mel Brooks, producer of the show *Springtime for Hitler*, found humor to be "just another defense against the universe."

Quincy Jones, modern music composer, record, and film producer, said, "I've always thought that a big laugh is a really loud noise from the soul saying, 'Ain't that the truth.'"

Darlene Greb, on learning I was writing about her in *Google Brain*, warned me, "Gordon, if you dare to put me in that book I'm going to stop cooking."

Well, I knew that ancient Greek women had tried stopping a war by denying their men sex. But refusing to cook is a new one. Shortly after our wedding I came home from work and found my new bride reading a collection of recipes. It was a wedding present, a cookbook called, *If You Can Read, You Can Cook.*

In checking out my wife's mother, I missed the fact that Mrs. Alcock couldn't cook. But luckily her daughter turned out to be a terrific reader!

GOOGLE GUIDE

Chapter 23: A Philosopher Learns to Laugh

For more on this subject, try these:

"Monty Python – Meaning of Life (Fighting Each Other)." (film).
Find title at YouTube: http://www.youtube.com/

"A Writer's Philosophy of Life," by Gordon Greb (text).
http://grebphilosophy.blogspot.com/

"Robert Benchley...That Inferior Feeling" Robert Benchley (1940)."
(film). Time: 9:08 min. Find title at YouTube: http://www.youtube.
com/

For a longer listing, go to the book's web site:

Google Brain Book: http://googlebrainbook.blogspot.com/

Chapter 24

I'm a Yankee Doodle Dandy

It's very easy to find something you're not looking for.

——Leo Rosten (1908-1997)

When you're accustomed to having a good relationship with the police, it comes as a shock when you find government authorities tapping your phone lines, surveying your mail, and tagging you as a suspicious character. To find this out in my own country, where you've always assumed you were as American as apple pie, was what made it personally shocking to me when it began happening during the Cold War.

During the stressful time starting a half century ago, especially during the anti-Viet Nam war protest movement during the 1960s, the anxiety over there being enemies in our midst caused the government to initiative police surveillance far and wide, reaching such a point that it was attempting to catch me and lots of other perfectly innocent people.

Learning the authorities were spying on me came as an astonishing surprise, because I was openly teaching students at San Jose State that democratic government was superior by showing the faults of living in a police state, one of the major characteristics of a communist or fascist system. Furthermore I came under suspicion because I was researching material on different political systems for a television course originating from the college's Instructional Television Center. But when the FBI found out that I'd been collecting communist literature, it got suspicious.

My interest in foreign propaganda methods began before World II. I started transcribing on discs the shortwave broadcasts from England,

172

Germany, Russia, and Japan in 1939, fascinated by each country's attempts to propagandize Americans. Saving these transmissions was made possible because my parents bought me a new Silvertone AM/SW radio, phonograph, and disc recording machine.

Immediately after the Japanese struck Pearl Harbor, the University of California began to explore ways its faculty could contribute to the war effort and approved the introduction of new courses designed to prepare students for responsibilities that would soon be theirs. I enrolled in "Military Intelligence" after learning this course would be taught by a team of experts from a variety of departments. One of the instructors was General David Prescott Barrows, intelligence head of the American forces when they tried to help the "White Army" overthrow the Russian communist government at the end of the First World War. Being a G-2 officer in that war, he came out of retirement as a former president of the university to help teach this course.

To qualify for the course, it required permission of the instructor and the issuance of an ID card to be admitted to the classroom each day. Furthermore we were told not to discuss what we were doing with outsiders and to keep everything we learned confidential. The aim of the course was to teach us how to collect and analyze information no matter where it came from. What we learned was how to uncover hidden truths. We were told it could be found anywhere, even in classified advertising. We were told not to overlook the tiniest detail. So it wasn't long after this intensive training program got underway that I realized this was one of the most stimulating and interesting courses I'd ever had.

For example, our attention was called to a book written by a young Japanese military officer, which had been published two years before December 7,1941. In the English translation he told how Japan could effectively cripple the United States with a surprise attack on Pearl Harbor. This was a perfect illustration of overlooked intelligence and we were told, "Too often what you need to know might be right there in front of your face and you don't see it. It's your job as an intelligence officer to see that that never happens."

While never formally assigned to the intelligence branch during my three years in the army, I learned after the war that several of my classmates did get such assignments, a few ending up in Wild Bill Donovan's Office of Strategic Services to be dropped off as spies behind enemy lines to carry out secret missions. Due to my being weak in foreign languages, I found myself assigned to other information processing and gathering duties.

After the war I remained interested in analytic studies and resumed them at the University of Minnesota as a graduate student, completing several academic papers on propaganda techniques under the direction of Dr. Ralph Nafziger, who had served as an information specialist with the U. S. military during the war. Recognizing the immense research value of what the government was having him do, he arranged for all the materials of the Foreign Broadcast Intelligence Service to be deposited in the University of Minnesota library and he made it personally available to me.

What I found during this course was amazing. Now available for postwar research were daily English translations of every short-wave broadcast that originated from the U.S.S. R., Germany, Japan, and the United Kingdom during the entire conflict. Using the techniques of content analysis, which Nafziger had taught me, I uncovered the methods Germany had tried to apply to "split the allies" during the war. These conclusions remain valid today in both of the unpublished papers I wrote in 1949. These papers of mine were: "Reply from Goebbels: How German shortwave radio used information from Allied sources for Propaganda," and "An analysis of the theme, 'A Second Front,' in German radio propaganda, before and after its military defeat in North Africa."

Later, during the Cold War, I was studying foreign propaganda, using every available source, searching through the literature in the library, exchanging correspondence with experts in the field, and making personal inspection tours whenever possible. Taking a six-month sabbatical leave in 1963, I traveled to foreign broadcasting stations all over Europe to study their operations. One of those trips had me driving my new 1963 Volkswagen bus through the Iron Curtain—my wife and seven-year old son scared to death in the back seats—to reach West Berlin to talk to American experts running our propaganda radio station there.

What caused me to believe the FBI had me under surveillance happened quite by accident. In the course of gathering materials by mail from the U.S.S.R. and its satellites in countries like Czechoslovakia, Poland, and Yugoslavia, agents of the Federal Bureau of Investigation apparently became interested enough to place a "cover" on my mail.

Someone must have thought that I was engaged in some kind of suspicious activity. I knew none of this was going on until I changed my place of residence, moving across town to a new home in San Jose, and then notifying everyone concerned of my "change of address," forgetting only one—an oil company with which I held a credit card.

When sometime later the Union Oil Company failed to get paid because its bills were no longer being forwarded, my delinquency was turned over to a collection agency which, without too much difficulty, found me at my new address and arranged payment. But because the U. S. Post Office would not—as its customary practice—forward mail after a certain lapse of time, I began to wonder why it had made at least one exception. Anything sent to the old address should already have gone into the "dead letter" file and when that happens you never know about it unless, as happened in this case, it's an overdue bill called to your attention by a collection company.

That's why it seemed unusual when I received a large brown envelope from Czechoslovakia Radio (behind the Iron Curtain) sent to my previous address long after I'd moved. This caused me to think, "Hey, this is funny. Why would the U.S. Post Office forward this piece of foreign mail from a communist country and not send me bills from the Union Oil Company in the good old USA?"

Then the possible reason dawned on me. The FBI had an office at the main post office. It must have been covertly opening everything sent me from behind the Iron Curtain and then forwarding it in order not to arouse my suspicions. Could you possibly think otherwise?

If you have any doubts, check me out for yourself. Simply go online to YouTube (www.youtube.com) and use its search engine to find the interview I did for television, called, "Cold War Revisited – 1961." What you'll see will be an eight-minute interview I conducted with a young Russian girl, Nina Kordowski, who tells frankly and fully what she thinks of a system of government that spies on you. In the case she described, it's communism.

This comes from a kinescope film taken of one of the lectures I gave at San Jose State on *The American Newspaper* in 1961 when I compared the press in the U.S.S.R. and Red China with that in the United States and Western Europe. In case you still have any doubts and still believe the FBI should subject me to a bit of water boarding to get at the truth, don't do anything till you see and hear what I plan to do next on YouTube, which is to sing my favorite song:

> *I'm a Yankee Doodle Dandy*
> *A Yankee Doodle, do or die*
> *A real live nephew of my Uncle Sam*
> *Born on the Fourth of July*
> *I've got a Yankee Doodle sweetheart*
> *She's my Yankee Doodle joy*
> *Yankee Doodle came to London*
> *Just to ride the ponies*
> *I am that Yankee Doodle Boy*
> (APPLAUSE)

Thank you, ladies and gentlemen, and thank you, too, George M. Cohan for expressing my feelings exactly with that stirring song you wrote!

GOOGLE GUIDE

Chapter 24: I'm a Yankee Doodle Dandy

For more on this subject, try these:

"Yankee Doodle Dandy 1942 Trailer." (movie trailer). Find title at YouTube: http:// www. youtube.com/

"Cold War Revisited," by Gordon Greb (film). Time: 8:51 min. http:// googlebrainbook.blogspot.com

"JibJab.com – This Land." (animated cartoon). http:// www.youtube.com/watch?v=z8Q-RdV7SY&feature=related/

For a longer listing, go to the book's web site:

Google Brain Book: http://googlebrainbook.blogspot.com/

Chapter 25

How I Quit Smoking

Habit is a habit, and not to be flung out of the window by any man,
but coaxed downstairs, one step at a time.

——Mark Twain (1835-1910)

Cigarettes, liquor, and wild, wild women. They weren't going to get me because I could remain aloof, strong, and self-controlled. But when temptation finally hit, it grabbed me, wrestled me to the ground, and turned me into a perfect idiot.

For years and years, everybody was doing it. So why not me? You saw it nearly everywhere—at work, in restaurants, trains, cars, and among your friends. In my own mind—thanks to advertising—I imagined myself a sophisticated, deep thinking intellectual, and a make- believe man of the world when I smoked. If you seriously thought about becoming a success, you had to have a cigarette, particularly if you wanted to attract the opposite sex.

If you don't know how romantic it can be to light up a Lucky Strike for someone of the opposite sex, go see the movie *Now Voyager*. See how appealing it looks when Paul Henreid lights up two cigarettes, one for himself and another for Bette Davis. Or find out how Hollywood studios made *Gilda* appealing. They did it with one of the sexiest posters of all time: Rita Hayworth, leaning seductively to one side, a come-on look on her face, and smoke from a cigarette curling up from one hand. That was enough to drive Glenn Ford crazy. But you ain't seen nothin' yet!

Now a Word from Our Sponsor

(A TV COMMERCIAL FROM THE 1950s)

CLOSEUP: Camel Cigarette Package

SLIDES: (Movie star photos)

ANCR: Many of Hollywood's brightest stars are Camel smokers—Tony Curtis, Jane Greer, John Wayne, and this lovely young lady, Maureen O'Hara, who finds that Camels' mildness and flavor agrees with her. Other Camel smokers are Marge and Gower Champion, that dynamic star Alan Ladd, and one of the newest favorites, Paramount's Charlton Heston.

ANCR: Mr. Heston, what especially do you like about Camels?

HESTON: Well, I don't know anything about the scientific tests various cigarettes claim or any of the things they say they have. I just know I like the taste of Camels. I find them very mild for me, too.

ANCR: Yes, America's smokers have shown an overwhelming preference for Camels. According to the latest published figures, Camels leads the second place brand by 43 per cent, the third place brand by 54 per cent and the fourth place brand by 144 per cent. Try Camels yourself and see what you've been missing.

Back Now to Our Program

With everybody doing it, it wasn't hard to picture myself as being a smart, good looking guy and almost as attractive as a Hollywood movie star. In actuality I was a poor imitation of the Marlboro man, regularly falling off his horse, and coughing and wheezing my way into an early grave. Living in that dream world, I was addicted to cigarette smoking for more than thirty years.

Only when I couldn't quit did it finally dawn on me that I was desperately in need of help. It wasn't till my health declined and general sense of well being began to disappear that the truth finally penetrated my thick skull. I'd become a slave of the devil, behaving in a most harmful way, and would surely go to hell if I didn't break free.

At the time I became addicted to the smoking habit at the age of twenty-two, it was already too late for me to hope for any kind of religious salvation. Evangelical saviors like the forceful Billy Sunday and Aimee Semple McPherson were gone from the national scene—the last of the great fighters against perdition and demon rum in the early twentieth century—who succeeded and then failed with Prohibition. In Billy Sunday's fight against alcohol, he convinced crowds gathered in auditoriums that they were sinners and with his convincing oratorical skills sent them home as saints.

While my addiction was to tobacco, not alcohol, I would have gladly quit drinking orange juice if it could have helped me break the habit of smoking. In desperation I'd have accepted assistance of any kind and from any source. Since I'd tried everything and nothing seemed to work, I decided to act like an educated man and read up on the subject.

Oddly enough I'd been alerted to its dangers before. That's when I'd been given an early warning by Carl Stover, a fellow graduate student at Stanford, who had stumbled across published research in the library showing clear evidence that smoking caused lung cancer. All of us teaching assistants had no difficulty finding this scientific paper.

I studied it carefully. But being young, happy and healthy, its message hardly made a blip on my radar screen. This paper, which was a single piece of research, stood alone and could have been an anomaly. I'd read of no other warnings in newspapers or magazines. Nearly all my friends were smoking in the 1950s and they all looked fine to me. So why worry?

Twenty years later, however, the world had changed. By the 1970s new research was clearly proving the dangers of smoking and the general public was being alerted to its harm. Then one day something came to my attention that hardly could be ignored since it came from my eight-year old daughter. She came home one afternoon with startling news, announcing, "Daddy, I just learned in school you shouldn't be smoking. My teacher says it hurts your health. Mommy thinks you should give it up, and I do, too. Won't you, please?"

Here it was—the strongest and most compelling reason to do anything— something I should do for my family and children. But I couldn't willy-nilly make a promise and not keep it. As Shakespeare observed in Hamlet, "it is a custom more honored in the breach than the observance." So I tried to level with my daughter, saying, "You're right. I really shouldn't smoke. But habits are sometimes very hard to break. For your sake, Daddy will try." With that, she smiled and went skipping away.

Now what was I to do? I'd tried one time earlier and failed, following the advice of one of the experts, who guaranteed readers, "My book will show you how to kick the smoking habit or you'll get your money back." Persuaded by this author's promise, I rushed to read what he advised, endured the suffering needed to carry out his advice, and after achieving success, made a mistake that caused the entire enterprise to fall into pieces.

After I'd been bragging to everyone for weeks—"You're looking at a man who's quit"—I was having a wonderful time at a party, was offered a cigarette, and unhesitatingly accepted, saying to myself, "Taking one cigarette now won't matter because I have great will power. I can quit anytime I want." Before the festivities ended, I had rewarded myself with one or two more cigarettes to celebrate such a remarkable achievement.

What a numbskull. Next day I found myself back at work, among fellow smokers, and felt the need for at least one more smoke. So I began "bumming" from colleagues until it got embarrassing. Then realizing this borrowing made me look like a cheapskate, I decided to buy a pack of cigarettes to keep in my desk drawer to use as needed. But somehow that package of Lucky Strikes got transferred from the office to my pocket, and I was puffing away again.

How was I ever to stop? Cursory reading of psychology books by William James, B. F. Skinner, and Norman Cousins gave me ideas on how it could be done. While not a trained psychologist, I felt a strong need to resolve this inner conflict one way or another. Which was strongest—my desire to smoke or desire to quit? I needed the answer for my own self-respect and it called for a careful analytic study of the question of why I was doing it.

So I sat down before a sheet of paper, drew a line down the middle, and began making a list of all the "good" and "bad" reasons I could think of for behaving one way or the other, which looked like this:

What's Good About Smoking?

- It made you feel relaxed, lighting up, and blowing smoke into the air.
- I could stop for a few minutes to get away from the world.
- When others are doing it, I didn't feel isolated but part of a group.
- It went well with a cup of coffee, a glass of wine, or after a good meal.
- It shut out noise and let me concentrate.
- Smoking made me feel comfortable while reading, writing, or driving.

What's Bad About Smoking

- Smoking was wrecking my health and sending me to an early grave.
- I was unnecessarily nervous and irritated when I didn't have a cigarette.
- My body and clothing stank of tobacco smoke everywhere I went.
- I worried that a carelessly tossed a cigarette could start a fire.
- When I didn't have a cigarette and had to beg, I felt like a bum
- I hated the sight of "No Smoking" signs.
- I was tired of emptying filthy, stinking ashtrays.
- Smoking was an expensive habit that made corporations richer and me, poorer.

- If I couldn't quit, that meant I'd become an addict and no longer a free person.
- After studying both lists, I knew which side had won, but the problem remained—how could I quit the habit once and for all?

Figuring Out a Plan to Quit

My grand strategy was to stop slowly, by reducing the smoking environments one by one. So I went about creating allowable smoking zones, ranking them in order as follows: the automobile, the office, the desk, home, easy chair, and so forth. Then gradually reducing the list of permissible places until there was only one place left.

This proved easy. Starting off I resolved to quit smoking in my car commuting back and forth to work. A few days later I quit smoking at faculty meetings which eliminated some more. Next I ruled out smoking in the family room while watching television and later nearly every room of the house. Soon I was smoking only half a pack and my anxiety level remained calm because there always was a place left to smoke if I waited long enough.

At the end of a couple of weeks, I found myself having to go to a single, designated chair in order to smoke. By this time there was such little nicotine left in my body I was able to say to myself, "This is ridiculous. Why do I need this chair? I don't want to smoke. So I quit."

But the battle wasn't over. I expected a little voice would now begin whispering in my ear and congratulating me on my victory. Sure enough, he came with enticing words of praise.

LITTLE DEVIL: Oh, you're so wonderful. You deserve to be congratulated for what you've done with that strong will power of yours. You deserve an award. It's something you really need and desire. Since you can start and stop anytime you want, give yourself a treat. Go right now and celebrate with someone who has a nice Camel, Lucky Strike, Chesterfield or—?

LITTLE ANGEL: Devil, go away! No more of your cunning tricks. I know your persuasive ways and your twisted logic. Long ago I was taught—once bitten, twice shy—and I'm not going to swallow any of your baited hooks. Go away because you're wasting my time.

That's how I did it. While those enticing thoughts in my head may not have come from old Lucifer, or Mephistopheles, I knew they were coming. Also I now knew they were manipulations placed in my head by other human beings like myself who had ulterior motives. To quit, you needed to decide for yourself.

Thank goodness thousand of others like me also recognized the profit-making devices of the tobacco industry and decided to do something about it. They voted to put a high tax on cigarette smoking to keep the devil away from our door. That now helps pay for public service advertising and programs that help keep people from starting a habit that never did anybody any good.

Whenever I see a poor soul puffing away on a cigarette outside of an office or grocery store, I'm tempted to approach the person and say, "Brother, you've been caught by the Devil and are going to hell. Let me save you from perdition—."

That's what I feel like doing. I have a strong desire to be like the evangelist Billy Sunday, who saved hundreds of thousands from the addiction of alcohol. To get started, I would need to rent a hall, pass out literature, collect donations, and prepare sermons to save these sinners from the evils of smoking with my oratory.

Has anybody seen today's "For Rent" section of the newspaper? Or shall I go to Craigslist? I need to rent a hall.

GOOGLE GUIDE

Chapter 25: How I Quit Smoking

For more on this subject, try these:

"Tex Williams Smoke Smoke Smoke (That Cigarette)." (song).
Find title at YouTube: http://www.youtube.com/

"The Golden Age of Cigarette Advertising." (film). Time: 3:01 min.
Find title at YouTube: http://www.youtube.com/

"Billy Sunday Preaching About Alcohol." Billy Sunday. (sermon).
Time: 2:22 min. Find title on YouTube: http://www.youtube.com/

For a longer listing, go to the book's web site:

Google Brain Book: http://googlebrainbook.blogspot.com/

Chapter 26

Welcome to the Twenty-First Century

There are three stages of life: youth, middle age, and "you're looking good."

——Anonymous

What's life like for octogenarians these days?

Here's the timeline from our Day Book:

6:00 am: Bedside radio awakens me and the cat with NPR news.

7:00 am: My wife Darlene opens one eye, squints at sunlight, and turns over.

7:30 am: Maybe one of us gets up. Then we spend a half-hour taking pills.

8:00 am: At last we're wide-awake, eat breakfast, and read the paper.

10:00 am: Too much reading, eyes tired, now sleepy. Can I go back to bed?

11:00 am: Dozing difficult due to barking dog, garbage man, and etc.

12 noon: Hey! It's lunchtime. What's it going to be? Flip a coin. Open a can.

1:00 pm: Wife must go shopping and says, "You drive and pay for the gas."

2:00 pm: Postman delivers mail—all advertising—not one First Class letter.

3:00 PM: What's the news? Tune on *BBC World Service, CNN,* something!!!

4:00 PM: News today is very upsetting. Give me a Pepcid, TUM, anything!

5:00 PM: Didn't anyone feed cat? She's clawing up our sofa she's so mad.

6:00 PM: Catastrophe. No TV dinners in fridge. Phone for a pizza.

7:00 PM: Jim Lehrer on PBS calms us, everything OK (the experts say).

8:00 PM: *Turner Classic Movies*—"All those stars look so young."

9:00 PM: Phone keeps ringing, telemarketers asking for money.

10:00 PM: Late news is terrible. Turn it off! Now we're wide-awake!

11:00 PM: What an exhausting day! Brush teeth. Take medicine. Rest.

12:00 AM: "Are you still awake?"

1:00 AM: "Yes, are you?"

2:00 AM: "Maybe we should throw off a blanket?"

3:00 AM: "That didn't work. Now I'm cold."

4:00 AM: Awakened by phone ringing "Sorry, wrong number."

5:00 AM: Snoring. Hard kick. Snoring stops.

6:00 AM: New crisis in the Middle East, according to NPR!

That's the way it's gone for most of the year. So what happens when you wake up some morning only to find your next-of-kin whispering, "Happy Birthday"? You're pretty sure she was whispering because you're too deaf to know if she was actually speaking louder than that! After feeling your pulse, you say to yourself, "Well, I'm still here."

You feel your wrist to find out if the ticker seems to be working. You open your eyes and peer dimly at walls, chairs, and various bedroom paraphernalia. You hear yourself saying, "I guess I'm still on terra firma" and reply to your bedmate (in a voice that is a barely a whisper), "Is that you, dear? I can't see the clock. What time is it?'

Wife: "Don't you know? It's later than you think! It's your big eight!"

Insignificant Other: "You mean it's eight o'clock already?"

Wife: "No, you big sleepy head. That's how old you are today. I'm supposed to light eighty candles for you today. But I'm not going to ruin a perfectly good chocolate cake with that many. Eight will have to do."

That's the reason you learn to laugh, as you grow older. If maturity comes with age, it's what you have to do. It's what you need to keep in mind when your wife thinks it's vitally important that you should see a doctor over what's been happening lately. She reminds you of having said the following:

(1) My hearing is improved. An audiologist has given me tiny, nearly invisible aids to stick in both ears. But the batteries go dead just when most politicians are about to speak. Yet I seem to know what they're going to say anyway. Is this a sign of something?

(2) My eyesight is improved. My ophthalmologist prescribed drops to impede the development of glaucoma. But every time I've thrown the bottle at the TV screen it hits a commentator squarely in the face without my needing to use a single drop. Is this a sign of something?

(3) My aching back is improved. My internist recommended using a portable, electrified pillow. But it vibrates so loudly during the news I can't hear anything or see anything a politician is saying even with closed captions. Still, this somehow relieves me from having a possible headache. Is this a sign of something?

(4) My attention deficit problem is improved. But my unwillingness to stay tuned to over-commercialized radio and TV and turning the sets off has created such a huge silence that I find myself shouting loudly and filling the room with so much non-stop grumbling and commentary that it forces my wife to go to another room. Is this a sign of something?

(5) Finally my automobile is broken down. When the mechanic learned that up to the last election I'd been having an increasing number of appointments to see my cardiologist, dentist, optometrist, ophthalmologist, internist, radiologist, clinicians, etc., he gave me a stern warning, "With all your driving around, your car isn't going to last much longer the way you're going."

Is this a sign of something?

Although I'm improved after the new remedies recently given to the body politic, my wife, after hearing all of that, thinks that I should contact a psychiatrist. But unless the good doctor makes house calls, I don't think it would do much good making an appointment. I can't afford to go anywhere these days anyway with the gasoline prices being what they are.

I'm really quite happy leaving things the way they are and will be perfectly contented as long as nobody messes with my funny bone. Being tickled to death is the only way to live.

Signed: A Recovering Academic.

GOOGLE GUIDE

Chapter 26: Welcome to the Twenty-First Century

For more on this subject, try these:

"New Years Eve 2000-2001 ABC – WBZ." (television).
Find title at YouTube: http://www.youtube.com/

"Looking Backward: 2000 – 1887," by Edward Bellamy. (book).
Find title at Google Books: http://books.google.com/

"Season's Greetings from a Golden Oldie," by Gordon Greb. (column). http://www.thecolumnists.com/greb/greb57.html/

For a longer listing, go to the book's web site:

Google Brain Book: http://googlebrainbook.blogspot.com/

Chapter 27

The Man Who Would Be King

Republicans are the party that says government doesn't work,
and then they get elected and prove it.

——P. J. O'Rourke (1947-)

My credentials for advice giving are outstanding. Experience and wisdom are written all over me. Warren G. Harding occupied the White House when I was born. I'm a survivor of the Great Depression, World War II, the Civil Rights Movement, and other crises too numerous to mention.

Wisdom gets knocked into your head pretty good after real-life experiences like those of the Anti-Vietnam War movement and the Gay Liberation Day parades in San Francisco. So I must warn you not to leap to any conclusions about what I plan to do.

After many days and nights of listening to America's talk radio I've come to the conclusion resistance is vital. While avoiding the pitfalls of the right-wingers' new American Way of Life will not be easy, it's what we must do. Otherwise it means that self-satisfied conservatives will see that you're "outsourced" from your job, thrown into the street without health insurance, and find no more funds available at the unemployment office.

Undoubtedly you will find yourself being persuaded to behave like a rugged individualist, selling apples on the street corner. Why not? That was the basic training experience that prepared all our young men and women to win World War II (becoming Tom Brokaw's *The Greatest*

Generation) but only after Roosevelt's job programs restored their spirit. He put young people back to work in the Civilian Conservation Corps and made them physically fit by living and working to preserve the great outdoors of America.

While I needn't warn you of the coming difficulties, the fact is you'll need to take one side or the other. Your choice will be to join the opposition as an old fashioned naysayer or join the growing number of Americans who have become the born-again-compromisers.

While disheartened and disillusioned liberals will try to fight this inevitable future, hoping somehow these changes can be stopped, the fact is that America is headed for a presidential repeal of everything that was enacted long ago by Franklin Delano Roosevelt if conservatives have their way. Radical Republicans never cease to campaign for the political power to do what they want. Since they're forever trying to seize control of the White House, Congress, and the Supreme Court, it's time now to adjust to this new reality, and learn what to do when it happens. George Bush came close to ruining the country when he had that kind of power.

- He promised one thing in his speeches and did the other in practice.
- He pretended to believe in limited government and then proceeded to expand its powers.
- He claimed to stand for individual liberty and then secretly took it away.
- He preached fiscal responsibility in government and then recklessly ran up the national debt.
- He appointed political incompetents to high office and then blamed government for its inefficiency.

While occupying the White House, Bush never told us what he really intended to do but his actions told us what he wanted to get rid of—every law and program enacted during Roosevelt's New Deal—and what he succeeded in repealing helped bring on the calamities we're facing today and will continue to face in the future.

Bush embraced every crisis as a new means to power. Each gave him the excuse to take drastic action to defeat this terrible new enemy that threatened our very survival. Oh, did you think I was going to mention the Bush administration's escalating national debt or the growing trade imbalance, especially with China? No, George Bush's crystal ball told him—and everybody else he chose to talk to—that we were face-to-face with something far worse: the insecurity of Social Security!

Since the solution to this problem was so simple, according to Bush, it's a wonder Roosevelt didn't think of it first—privatization. The Bush administration, cheered along by Newt Gingrich and Rush Limbaugh, seriously proposed that taxpayers should be encouraged to take all the money they've accumulated in Social Security and invest it in Wall Street. They proposed to let each of us risk our savings— billions of our hard-earned dollars—in stocks, bonds, money market accounts, options, puts, calls, mutual funds, and investment deals of all kinds.

What a bonanza for Wall Street that would have been! What a brilliant idea. Each of us would collectively pay millions of dollars in commissions to brokers to put our retirement savings in the stock market and then risk losing everything if our investments went bad. It was a perfect scheme for someone like Bernard Madoff, now jailed for life for carrying out history's largest so-called Ponzi scheme with billions of dollars of other people's money. But how do you suppose Donald got to the top floor of the Trump Tower? Borrowed money, that's how. So why not you?

I'd already experimented with what Bush was proposing long ago. I began investing in the stock market 60 years ago. That's when the Dow Jones average was below 500 and three million was the average number of shares traded in a day. Yes, I can hear you saying, "This guy must be rich!"

Being Mr. Average Investor I bought a book explaining how to do it but had no idea what to buy. My choices became Southern Pacific Railroad, Kaiser Pemanente Cement, and Peabody Coal. For weeks and months they just sat there and stared at me on the financial pages, going nowhere. In my ignorance I was willing to be guided by a so called investment counselor with Dean Witter, who made matters even worse (for me, not him).

I never realized a penny of profit with all this buying and selling. I found out investing is a full-time job and not for amateurs. What saved me from bankruptcy was Joe, my barber, who advised me to buy

Sheraton Hotels. In the 1950s in San Jose, this guy was buying houses (on credit) and reselling them (at a higher price).

I made enough money from his advice to offset the losses on what my broker was getting me into. Finally I sold out, was happy to come out even, and spent my savings on a three-month trip to Europe. That was the wisest investment I've ever made. It gave me rich and valuable experiences and let me live for a while like a rich American on five dollars per day.

So I thank heaven that George Bush's plan to privatize Social Security never took place. Since so many true believers in the Bush ideology continue to blindly oppose Roosevelt's New Deal—the program that helped make America great during the past sixty years—it seems useless to try to argue even after the stock market crash of 2008.

Instead of trying to fight the propaganda machine from the Bush White House, I decided to return to the life of a "rugged individualist" and cut my personal spending program—saving every penny coming in for a rainy day. Although I may seem that I'm trying to become a financial giant like Warren Buffet, here are some examples of "My Personal Economy Measures to Survive as a Private Individual in America":

- I'm started saving hundreds of dollars by canceling cable TV (using the free antenna).
- I buy only low-priced, secondhand records, cassettes, DVDs, and CDs.
- I chose to drive my 2005 Toyota Camry that gets 35 miles to the gallon instead of my old 1997 gas-guzzling SUV.
- I cut up "junk mail" into scratch pads instead of tossing this useable paper into the garbage can.
- My list is too long to itemize here but Benjamin Franklin had the right idea when he said, "A penny saved is a penny earned."

Did I prepare myself for the Bush's Great Recession? As someone old enough to remember the Great Depression, the answer is obvious. As soon as Bush took office in 2001, the future was clear. It seemed inevitable we'd repeat the stock market collapse of 1929 with neo-conservatives in power.

My strategy was to wait for the panic! That's when I'd look for bargains in the stock market and not a day sooner. Maybe privatization of Social Security didn't finally happen under the Bush administration. But conservative scare tactics will be tried again and again. That's why for the entire twentieth century we were the only great nation in the world without adequate medical care for all our people.

When members of Generation X finally wake up to what following the Pied Piper of Privatization really means, we'll see whether it pleases these followers of the radical conservative theory in the long run. They'll be headed for a new survivor show not likely to be seen on television because it will be taking its creators along with it.

GOOGLE GUIDE

Chapter 27: The Man Who Would Be King

For more on this subject, try these:

"George Bush on Social Security." (CNBC cable).
Find title at YouTube: http://www.youtube.com/

"The Man Who Would be King," by Stuart Taylor Jr. (article).
Atlantic Monthly, April 2006.
http://www.theatlantic.com/doc/200604/bush-autocracy/

"Halloween on Wall Street," by Gordon Greb. (column).
http://www.thecolumnists.com/greb/greb54.html/

For a longer listing, go to the book's web site:

Google Brain Book: http://googlebrainbook.blogspot.com/

Chapter 28

Is Orwell's 1984 Here Already?

Today is the tomorrow we worried about yesterday!

——Tom Wilson (1931-)

I have a confession to make. I was considerably worried all the time George W. Bush occupied the White House. Day after day he left me feeling very uncomfortable with everything he was doing. As an example of my concern, let me tell you how I was feeling in February 2005. Up to that time I'd never been afraid to make a telephone call but that's what got it started.

Everything seemed to be pretty normal around the house and neighborhood that morning. It was quiet and peaceful. For someone growing up after the stock market crash of 1929 and trying to survive the 20th Century, nobody and nothing up to that time could possibly have really scared me unless it was Dr. Frankenstein himself. Then I found things happening that reminded me of what George Orwell had predicted years ago. It came without warning. Ye, gads! I discovered the forewarning in his book *1984* was now coming true.

During the early 1930s the nation was in deep economic trouble, but President Roosevelt never covered it up, saying, "... Only a foolish optimist can deny the dark realities of the moment." He said we would solve these problems and those of us who found employment believed he did. Since those days, having lived through crises of many kinds—gangsters, wars, inflation, injustice, prejudice, riots, and corruption—

I've always felt confident we could find a way to deal with them and had nothing to fear.

But all that changed with this particular phone call. My shock came from dialing the wrong 800-telephone number. What I got on the other end suddenly convinced me that the movie *Metropolis*—that remarkable 1926-look-into-the-future by movie director Fritz Lang—was much closer than we thought.

For years I'd referred to my personal computer as "Hal," which was a tribute to Stanley Kubrick's imaginative view of the twenty-first century in his classic film, *2001: A Space Odyssey.* Whether you're using a PC or a Mac today, strange things happen to make you believe computers have minds of their own. After dialing this wrong number in this particular case, I got a voice that sounded like a robot from Star Wars named R2D2. By mistakenly dialing, 1-888-123-4567, this is what I got:

RECORDING

Welcome. You've reached the special relations unit of your behind-the-scenes government. Thank you for calling The Confidential Big Brother Contributions and Bribery Office to help us advance the idea of free enterprise in public service and learn how you may be rewarded for it.

Since all of our operators are busy, please punch the appropriate number. If you are a radio, TV, or print journalist wishing to apply for one of our special under-the-table contracts, please select one of the following:

- To use one of our controversial publicity releases word-for- word as your own in a bylined column, article, program or newscast, choose 1.
- To slip the propaganda we supply you into work of one of your colleagues, choose 2.
- To help us lambaste opponents with our ideas which you'll put into your own work, choose 3.

- To attend news conferences using questions we've told you to ask in advance of our officials and publish their answers word-for-word, choose 4.
- To speak with an operative about any new or novel bribery ideas of your own, please stay on the line.

On hearing this, I was speechless. Here was a chance to join the crowds making off with tons of legal tender from the U.S. Treasury Department in Washington, D.C.—a way to make loads of money from the George W. Bush administration. All I had to do was agree to slip the Bush administration views into the column I was writing online, and make certain its contents always conveyed good news about the current administration. What an easy way to make money!

Everyday you read or hear about millions of dollars being given to heads of corporations, slick politicians, brokerage firm dealmakers, golden-parachuters, etc. Now journalists could get in on it. Why shouldn't I? That was my thinking when a voice came on the line:

VOICE: Are you a writer, journalist, newsman, or someone who has a following in the media?

GREB: Well ... ah ...Yes, I do write a column.

VOICE: Good. We like columnists. How many readers do you have?

GREB: I really don't know. But my editor thinks we could get plenty of advertisers for the asking. Would you like to be considered an advertiser?

VOICE: No. These are special arrangements with your government that are now kept secret. But we're good people with good intentions. We're like patrons of Italy who supported great art in the past, which, as you know successfully pictured kings, queens, and members of the royal court in wonderful colors. It's been a great conservative tradition.

GREB: Sounds great to me. What do I do and how do I get paid?

VOICE: It's simple. You'll receive a call from one of our departments—say, for example, Education or Defense—and you tell them you agree to a verbal contract. After this, they'll reward you with an educational project that will pay you handsomely—sometimes as much as one hundred thousand dollars an assignment. It depends on how many jobs you do. Carry them out and as soon as your columns are published, you'll be paid immediately with under-the-counter cash.

GREB: This is great. Sign me up. Dr. Samuel Johnson once said, "Nobody writes for free except blockheads."

VOICE: One last thing. How did you vote in the November election?

GREB: Why do you need to know that?

VOICE: I'm surprised you don't know. This administration always maintains quality control. During the last campaign, everyone attending a presidential speech had to be screened and hold a ticket issued by us.

GREB: What if I told you I voted for Bush and didn't.

VOICE: Oh, that's impossible. We know how everyone voted. Nearly all of our voting machines are programmed to track how everybody votes. We'd know.

GREB: Then if I told you I'd voted for the Democratic candidates, you'd be able to find that out and consider that a terrible mistake?

VOICE: If that's your admission, we certainly can confirm it. If it's not in our computer records, then we'd verify it through water boarding. But since you've already confessed your guilt, you certainly are not qualified for a bribery contract. Therefore we're adding your name to Nixon's enemies list and notifying liberal treason investigator Ann Coulter to keep you under surveillance. Now that we're fully alerted, this ends our conversation.

CLICK: (abrupt phone disconnection)

Since I dialed this secret government office accidentally, I was unable to call back to persuade this slush-funder to give me a bribery contract. So today I remain a poor columnist. Yes, a "blockhead" looking for new and novel ways to make money.

Bribery, for the moment, is definitely out of the question.

GOOGLE GUIDE

Chapter 28: Is Orwell's 1984 Here Already?

For more on this subject, try these:

"1984 By George Orwell, 1949." (Planet eBook).
http://www.planetebook.com/1984.asp/

"Newspeak from the Recent Attacks 2001-09-13." (Newspeak dictionary). http://www.newspeakdictionary.com/ns_frames.html/

"It's the 'New' Old World: March 14, 2005," by Gordon Greb. (column). http://www.thecolumnists.com/greb/greb12.html/

For a longer listing, go to the book's web site:

Google Brain Book: http://googlebrainbook.blogspot.com/

Chapter 29

Lord, Give Me My Daily Paper

*If one morning I walked on top of the water across the Potomac River,
the headline that afternoon would read: PRESIDENT CAN'T SWIM.*

——Lyndon B. Johnson (1908-1973)

The sun was hardly up. Fortunately, I was up early, having my breakfast alone, and nobody around to hear me grumbling to myself over my toast and coffee. I had dashed out the front door to pick up the morning paper and it wasn't there. This was more than disquieting. It was terribly upsetting because reading the paper has been such a vital part of my life all these years.

Back in the good old days—which few people remember today—the humorist who spoke common sense to the American people was Will Rogers, who said, "All I know is what I read in the newspapers."

Who in today's generation has the slightest understanding of what he meant? We've trained so many people into believing that everything they need to know comes from computers, cellular telephones, and similar push-button gadgets that they now think it quaint to read the daily paper for news and information these days.

But satisfied moderns overlook one important fact: electronic news is not yet gathered, written, or edited by robots. It doesn't magically appear from cyberspace but comes from the hard work of reporters and editors. News requires flesh and blood human beings to go forth every day to find out and report what is happening.

When newspapers fail, there will be no news feed for any electronic media to pick up and deliver. A democratic society still needs professional reporters to go forth into the world and bring back what they find—from local police departments and city halls to the offices of kings, prime ministers, and presidents. We've always trusted they'd do it well and most of the time they haven't failed us.

Will Rogers was right then and right today: The news you get today depends almost entirely on newsgathering by journalists working for the print press. That news delivery system began five hundred years ago and not much has changed, despite the invention of radio, television, computers, and the Internet, except the means of delivery.

For an entire lifetime I've had a habit of opening my newspaper each morning as though it were some wonderful present from Santa Claus under my Christmas tree or a surprise gift on my birthday. That's why no newspaper at my doorstep this morning was terribly upsetting. I had, as usual, dashed out the front door in my pajamas—hoping no neighbor would see me—in that wet and chilly early morning dawn. When it wasn't there, I said loud and clear, "Nobody is going to steal my newspaper. If it's gone, I want to know why."

A shudder ran down my spine remembering what had been troubling me. Newspaper advertising revenues were declining. Circulation was falling. It was causing cutbacks of editorial staffs all over the country. Surely this didn't mean the end of papers, as I've known them? I dreaded the mere thought of losing good investigative reporting and keen analysis due to any crisis like this.

Even though I'm not responsible for what's happening, I can't help wrestling with the question, "How can we save these great newspapers?" There's nothing that I can see to replace them once they're gone. Our society, institutions, and culture need a free press. They've been good watchdogs of government and major institutions of society even before George Washington became our first president. They've barked loudly to alert the citizenry and made it possible for people to set things right before it was too late.

Now we live in a computer world. We're wired from one end of the earth to another. Satellites up high in the heavens beam down phone conversations, family photos, chat rooms, and tons of data on our command. Because we've been hyping the Internet as the coming thing, is it possible all this hoopla may have beguiled too many advertisers into being wooed away when it was not in their best interest to do so?

Although there's a proper niche in our lives for the Internet, the idea that it can completely replace the daily newspaper is ridiculous. Publishers got into a similar panic back in the early 1930s when radio came along. They feared radio's popularity would siphon off all the advertising from the print media. It was during the Great Depression. So publishers decided to boycott radio and ordered editors to pull the radio logs. When this had no apparent effect, they next tried owning and running radio stations. That didn't help either.

What finally saved newspapers was something surprisingly simple: they got increasingly better. That's what newspapers must do today. But they've forgotten why they became an important niche in our lives in the first place. Radio faced with competition from television discovered its niche. Television, too, when cable and satellite came along. They're all still with us. Now it's time for newspapers to reexamine their basic function and get back to doing it again in this new world of the Internet.

Much blame for the woes of newspapers is placed on our newly wired world. But is anybody evaluating what we're being fed? For example, it's assumed that measuring the huge numbers reading web pages is a good thing. A machine is tabulating those "hits" and making them seem significant. But where is the human brain evaluating what's being fed to us and whether all those hits really mean anything? Are robots trying to control everything we think and do as the computer Hal attempted in the movie *2001: A Space Odyssey*?

The survival of newspapers—like books—depends on developing young people who to love to read. But if we encourage them to read, what exactly will they be reading? My three young grandchildren are all readers, thanks to their having had books read to them from babyhood. Yes, these children love television, the movies, computers, and listening to music. Right now they also accompany their mother to the library to get books to read. But when they are older, who will advise them on what to read on the Internet? Publishers should be aware of what's happening in high schools and colleges because they have a role to play alongside teachers. They need to be pathfinders through the Web just as educators guide students through the world of knowledge.

I'm hoping that someday Silicon Valley will come up with a new gadget to help us integrate newspapers with the Internet. I envision holding a magic pen in my hand—something like a small wireless scanner mouse—to use when reading newspapers, books, magazines, and print media in the future. By using a little pen of that sort, I could scan the embedded URLs in what I'm reading on the printed page and have access later to recommended links to good movies, videos, DVDs, sounds, music, commentary, and text.

This guidance, of course, will depend on what I'll find on the printed page when the time comes to use this gadget. I'm depending on newspapers finally rediscovering their primary function and putting reporters on it. Hasn't that primary function been to serve as a "watch dog" of whatever is happening to our government and society? That needs to be done again in a new way. Newspapers must wake up, recognize their primary function, and start being a "watch dog" of the World Wide Web. Why aren't they telling us what we can trust or value on the Internet?

Daily papers have consistently reviewed plays, movies, books, television, business, sports, and nearly everything under the sun. But so far editors have missed covering the truly "big story"—the computer revolution itself. As it is, the Internet is behaving like a Wild West circus and sharp hucksters and pitch artists are out there trying to sell us medicine oil and get-rich-quick schemes. Where are the standard brands we can trust? Which gossipmongers and charlatans should we avoid? I think readers would subscribe to newspapers that regularly gave us expert judgment on what's worth viewing on their screens and what to avoid. While there's much good being pumped into the system, there's also much that's bad.

Who's better qualified to warn readers of swindles and scams on the Internet than experienced editors and reporters in the print media? For more than two centuries they've been observers and critics of society, government, sports, politics, and business in America and helped to guide us on our way. Until the print media recognize they have an important new role in this Age of the Internet and create special sections in their newspapers dealing with it, we're all going to be wasting our time trying to do it for ourselves.

How will we maintain good government and a decent society without newspapers? As Los Angeles police detective Joe Friday said on Dragnet, "We only want the facts, Ma'm." Gossip, opinion, and manufactured propaganda aren't enough. Without enterprising reporters and editors, dedicated to finding the truth and telling it as best they can, we lose what Thomas Jefferson valued most about the First Amendment to the United States Constitution—the people's right to know.

Thus my prayer is simply this, "Lord, please let me sit in the comfort of my easy chair, savoring a cup of coffee and chewing on a doughnut, to pick and choose what I want to read from my newspaper and then letting me go to my computer to get more sights, sounds, and expanded coverage, thanks to saved URLs taken from the pages of my newspaper."

Newspapers should be the place for the general public to find out what's right and wrong about we're being served on the Web. This "watchdog" institution is necessary and valuable to American society.

Ask yourself, would Will Rogers today be saying, "All I know is what I read on the Internet?" Editors, we need your help in finding our way through this labyrinth. Won't you please provide it?

GOOGLE GUIDE

Chapter 29: Lord, Give Me My Daily Paper

For more on this subject, try these:

"Bill Moyers: What's Wrong with Big Media." (video).
Find title at YouTube:http://www.youtube.com/

"Fame, My Son, is Not for Editors," by Gordon Greb. (article).
http://grebandson.blogspot.com/

"JibJab – What We Call the News." (animated cartoon).
Find title at YouTube: http://www.youtube.com/

For a longer listing, go to the book's web site:

Google Brain Book: http://googlebrainbook.blogspot.com/

Chapter 30

Walter Mitty, Cary Grant, and Me

A man who is high up loves to think that he has done it all himself,
and the wife smiles, and lets it go at that.

—J.M. Barrie (1860-1937)

A behind-the-scene look at "History's Mysteries," when the film crew came
to the author's home to make a program for the PBS network and stirred
things up a bit.

When movie star Cary Grant was told by an interviewer at one time, "Everybody would like to be Cary Grant," he is reported to have said, "So would I." Well, believe it or not, that's exactly what happened to me.

After months of negotiations, signing of contracts, choosing costumes, finalizing travel arrangements, the PBS crew came to my house to do the first "shoot" for an episode of the television series. They'd come to interview me about a "history mystery" I'd found and to see what kind of story it could tell. They were especially interested in something I'd pulled out of one of my old trunks.

When they walked through the front door with all of their equipment, I soon found myself on a set, co-starring with one of the most gorgeous young ladies I've ever seen outside of Hollywood. I'm not good at names but I think hers sounded like Eva Marie Saint. If you've seen this PBS show, you'll recognize her immediately. But for me, just meeting her caused something very unusual to happen. The trouble began with my being placed opposite her and being told by the director to keep staring straight into her perfectly lovely face.

Doing it seemed to cast a mysterious spell over me as this attractive woman kept smiling deliciously back at me. It was at that moment I couldn't help wondering, "Is this what Cary Grant had to endure making movies? How could he stand it?"

As everybody in Hollywood knows, in making a movie you often hear the expression, "Let's do another take." As the sound man adjusts his dials, the cameraman gets his lens in focus, and the director lines up the next "take," I'm told to sit as close as possible to this picture-perfect woman for nearly every scene being shot. Neither she nor I argued one bit about our close proximity to one another but it got to be so intimate that I couldn't help studying the attractive features of this young woman seated near me.

Ordered to remain this way for one take after another, I soon began to enjoy looking at the perfect contours of her face. As I studied it from every angle I got to know each and every one of its perfect features. I saw that she had wildly attractive brown eyes and lovely coiffured hair. A perky small nose. Rosy lips. Smooth skin. And perfectly shaped head, neck, and shoulders. Her voice was soothing and her attentive manner thrilling.

Over and over, we delivered our lines. The director never seemed satisfied. Whatever he wanted changed, he always insisted that we stay where we were, continue looking at each other, and to keep smiling. Right from the start the director turned to me and said, "I like your vitality."

The effect in this situation was mesmerizing. I had lots of time to think as the two of us stayed close together but after awhile it began to have a hypnotic effect on me. It seemed unbelievable but as this situation continued minute after minute, I felt more and more like Cary Grant in a one of his romantic movies.

I wanted to do what he did on the screen—grab her in my arms, whisper endearing words, and demonstrate to film audiences everywhere what it means to be a leading man. It's what Gary Grant does when he is thrown into the arms of a lovely star. He doesn't hesitate a second to prove to screen audiences everywhere that romance can be found anywhere, anytime, and at any age.

Memories of an old radio program came to mind. It was the daytime soap opera, *The Romance of Helen Trent,* and I recalled the voice of the announcer who told its listeners every day, "The Romance of Helen Trent is the story of a woman who sets out to prove what so many other women long to prove in their own lives—that romance can live on at thirty-five and even beyond."

Yes, I felt those words could apply to me—a guy named Cary Grant in place of Helen Trent—who has been looking for romance since he exceeded the age of thirty-five. And now this promise of romance was coming to me—someone much older than thirty-five to be sure—and who wanted for that moment to crash through the age barrier of the twenty-first century. But I hesitated for one moment, postponing immediate action, because in back of my mind was one little lingering doubt: "Was this really happening to me or someone else?"

Occasionally the Voice of Reality reminded me, "Gordon, you dumb bell, you're old enough to be this young woman's grandfather." But then another little voice urged me on, saying, "Forget the age differences. Opportunity only knocks once. Grab this girl, throw her into your fuel-efficient 2006 Toyota Corolla, and whisk her away like Charles Boyer or Richard Gere to Algiers to demonstrate how much you love her."

While all of this was going on in my head, my wife Darlene was in the other room. I realized she wouldn't like what I was thinking or wanting to do. I hoped that she would understand, having gone to school in Van Nuys with Marilyn Monroe and seeing first hand what kind of electricity was picked up by young, impressionable boys who bumped into the likes of pretty girls like Marilyn Monroe in the school hallways.

After entering the "studio" (our front room), Darlene look one look at the so-called shoot, watched the crew rearrange all of her furniture in her living room, and turning on her heel, walked out. She was totally unimpressed by what the film crew had moved and changed—the relocation of our lamps, tables, chairs, books, and even the huge television set. None of this was exciting to her. It was terribly disrupting!

No wonder! Darlene took one look at everything missing from the kitchen, breakfast room, and hallway that had been moved hither and yon to create a "new set" and walked away. She headed toward the back of the house that was the farthest distance away from this activity and announced, as she shut the door, "I'm going to read a book." In her hand she carried, *The Razor's Edge* by W. Somerset Maugham, whose principal theme was looking for the meaning of life.

This left me alone with the star. I was trying to ignore the fact this adorable female undoubtedly had a male associate back home with thoughts of his own and would probably want to punch me in the nose had he known mine. Although absent from the scene, I knew that if any other admirer of this young woman had seen at least one of Cary Grant's best movies, he would be ready *To Catch a Thief* the minute he discovered anything untoward was happening.

As for me, I was living for the moment. Being "on location" opposite this attractive woman, I couldn't help thinking about the kind of behavior Cary Grant demonstrated making movies with Irene Dunne in *The Awful Truth* and Ingrid Bergman in *Notorious*. As I continued to stare into my co-star's lovely brown eyes, I began to get a clearer idea of what Cary Grant actually would do in similar situations. Here was my chance to act like him and make this movie a box office bonanza. But I hesitated.

All my life I had wanted to be a movie star. "You ought to be in pictures" was sung on the radio when I was a kid growing up, usually by Rudy Vallee or the Boswell Sisters. I wondered if those lyrics would ever apply to me. That song came from the Ziegfeld Follies of 1934 and I kept hearing it in my head over and over as we were making this new movie.

But something else came to mind as well. I asked myself: Is it possible that I'm not actually Cary Grant in *That Touch of Mink* with Doris Day but really Tom Ewell in *The Seven Year Itch* with Marilyn Monroe? When Tom Ewell, a senior citizen, was left home alone by his wife, he got all hot and bothered over the femme fatale next door and imagined all sorts of romantic possibilities with her until the absent wife suddenly showed up and put a smashing end to all his stupid daydreaming. That was the end of Tom Ewell. He was last seen with Angela Lansbury in a 1986 episode of *Murder, She Wrote*.

Then again there was this problem of being Cary Grant. I began to realize he couldn't keep the same woman. He was constantly in real life stumbling into one romance after another. He never seemed satisfied, having been married five times—four of his wives having left him flat and walking out—Dyan Cannon, Betsy Drake, Barbara Hutton, and Virginia Cherrill.

What was the matter with Cary Grant? Couldn't he stay married? My daydreaming was interrupted by the director, who announced the lunch break.

"Okay, Gordon, where do we go?"

"Oh, I know a perfect place," I said. "It's my wife's favorite."

"Okay, get her and let's go."

Darlene came from the other room and led everyone down the street to a lovely little sandwich shop where I sat at a table with the director, my female co-star, and my wife. But the spotlight no longer was focused on me. It was now with these two women, who were happily engaged in animated conversation about the female star's two children and my wife's three grandchildren. These women were ignoring me completely!

This left me with only the director. So hoping to keep him thinking about me, I said, "Did you know *The Adventures of Robin Hood* starring Errol Flynn and Olivia de Havilland was made right here in Chico?"

"Wonderful picture," the director replied, swallowing a piece of his salad,

"What do you think of the idea of someone doing a remake of that old classic?" I asked.

"Great idea," he replied.

"Do you think we could get in touch with Olivia de Havilland?" I replied. "I'd love to work opposite her."

Lunch over, we returned to the set to finish shooting more scenes, inside and outside, which convinced me I really liked being in front of the camera. Would I like to star in a movie again? Why not? But I certainly wouldn't be interested in playing the role of the Sheriff of Nottingham in a remake of Robin Hood. I want to be Errol Flynn opposite Olivia de Havilland. No doubt about it!

Note: The story you have just read is absolutely true but names have been changed to protect the innocent. Because the author has been a lifetime admirer of *The New Yorker's* James Thurber, he hopes he has shown here that being like Walter Mitty could actually happen to anyone in real life.

GOOGLE GUIDE

Chapter 30: Walter Mitty, Cary Grant, and Me

For more on this subject, try these:

"The Secret Life of Walter Mitty [1]." (film). Time: 9:53 min. Find title at YouTube: http://www.youtube.com/

"Cary Grant: A Class Apart," by Graham McCann. (book). See quotation on page xi: "Everybody wants to be Cary Grant..." Find title at Google Books: http://books.google.com/

"Silents, Please!: Feb. 21, 2005," by Gordon Greb. (column). http://www.thecolumnists.com/greb/greb10.html/

For a longer listing, go to the book's web site:

Google Brain Book: http://googlebrainbook.blogspot.com/

Chapter 31

Who Was the Real Shakespeare?

[During a transatlantic crossing,] Einstein explained his theory to me every day and on my arrival I was fully convinced he understood it.

——Chaim Weizmann (1874-1952)

I love a mystery! I have such an insatiable curiosity that everything on earth seems interesting. I'm like a newborn babe fascinated by the face of my mother smiling down at me in the crib. The puzzles of life have posed so many questions for me to unravel that I've found myself forever chasing the answers like a dog after its tail.

Dining one night in San Francisco with a group of writers, well-known author and newspaper columnist Jerry Nachman turned to my wife, who was seated next to him, and politely asked, "Are you a writer, too?"

"No," she said with a confident smile. "I'm a reader, not a writer."

Where would we be, my friends, without readers? Would there be a single good reason to keep scribbling away or typing madly at a keyboard if there were no readers. My wife Darlene noticed recently in the *New York Times* that all of the best sellers in fiction were mysteries. That kind of popular interest goes back as far as Edgar Alan Poe's bone-chilling thrillers and Sir Arthur Conan Doyle's crime-solving detective series and probably originated with our human species. It's in our genes.

Whenever I find a good story, it plays upon this urge, arouses my curiosity, and gets me to turn pages in a book. As a matter of fact,

I'll bet right now you're wondering why I've brought up the question, "Who Was the Real Shakespeare?" The reason is simple. It explains why I became a professor and became addicted to research.

It all began when I became curious about my ancestry. My mother's maiden name was Benbow, a name quite similar to Shakespeare. Since the definition of Benbow was that of an archer who could bend the bow, I wondered whether we could possibly be related. The possibility led me to hunt down the origins of my ancestry and this search led me, as Alice would have said, down a rabbit hole that got "curioser" and "curisor" as I chased after the answer to the question, "Where did we come from?"

The mistake was that I started out concentrating on "Benbow" and not "Greb," a surname that resembled the mating call of a male frog in Walden Pond, trying to attract the attention of females by croaking, "greb … greb … greb." What my search finally turned up shouldn't have surprised me. It's exactly what happens to scientists focusing on a particular problem. When they start looking for a vein of coal in one direction, they end up finding diamonds in another.

"Ah, I see, Dr. Watson," I hear Sherlock Holmes saying in my imagination. "You've given me a new clue from this interesting collection of evidence." Then the great detective dashes to the door. Pausing only to light his long-stemmed pipe before bounding down the stairs, he says, "Hurry, Watson, we have no time to waste getting to the British Library. Put down that glass of Madeira and follow me. We have work to do."

On September 8, 2007, audiences in England saw the last performance of a controversial play, *I Am Shakespeare*, starring a cast of distinguished actors and actresses. The play presented evidence that the greatest works in the English language were not composed by the pen of the actor William Shakespeare but by someone much more talented, the strongest evidence pointing to Edward de Vere, the Earl of Oxford.

Well-known Shakespearean actors Derek Jacobi and Mark Rylance joined a growing number of literary scholars who've long expressed grave doubts that the actor from Stratford upon Avon was actually the creative genius behind those plays. Their suspicions were supported by two hundred modern day academics, and twelve hundred members of the Shakespeare Authorship Coalition. For more than a century, a number of prominent personages have felt that Shakespeare could not have written the plays. Among them were the following:

Mark Twain, author and humorist, who came to the conclusion that giving credit to Shakespeare, the actor, was built on a very thin foundation of inconsequential facts, guesses, inferences, theories, and conjectures.

Orson Welles, film actor and director, who asserted, " ...there are some awfully funny coincidences to explain away."

Charlie Chaplin, stage and screen star, who felt none of the sonnets and plays showed the slightest sign of the humble beginnings of the actor born at Stratford upon Avon.

Sigmund Freud, the psychiatrist, who refused to believe "the actor from Stratford" could have authored the greatest works in the English language.

Charles Dickens, novelist, whose great doubts led him to say, "Shakespeare is a fine mystery ..."

Walt Whitman, distinguished poet, who believed the plays were the work of "one of the 'wolfish earls' so plenteous in the plays themselves ... [not] the Avon man, the actor."

Many scholars now believe that what Shakespeare put on the stage actually were works from the pen of the Robert de Vere, the Earl of Oxford, who, for reasons of his own, felt it important for his own safety to keep his role in playwriting a secret. After all, he was a member of the court of Queen Elizabeth.

None of this really mattered to me until one day when I was browsing at a bookstore and made an accidental discovery of Elsdon C. Smith's *New Dictionary of American Family Names*. Much to my chagrin, "Benbow" wasn't in the book at all. But much to my surprise I found my surname "Greb" among the 2,180 surnames which were listed and whose origins had been traced.

What came as a complete surprise on opening the pages of this scholarly work was that my surname Greb was linked to all the royal courts of Europe and that it was linked to a very rich ancestry indeed. The dictionary defined my name as follows:

Greb, Grebe, Grebb (Ger.) *Variant of Graff, q. v.*

Graf, Graff (Ger., Fr., Eng.) *The earl or count; overseer in a lord's establishment; one who acted as a public scribe.*

I naturally was astonished, because it was like entering a "Time Machine" and suddenly meeting my forbearers. According to this peerage, my ancestors were both "scribes" as well as "earls." Since all the Shakespeare plays came from the pen of a scribe and are now believed the work of an earl, it was only logical for me to assume, "At last I've found my true inheritance." I must fly to Europe as quickly as possible to claim my rightful place in society.

Without hesitating, I gave my travel agent his instructions: Reserve two First Class tickets on British Airways to London. Have a driver with a limousine waiting for us at London's Heathrow airport and reserve the royal suite at the closest hotel to Buckingham Palace. Then "tweak" Queen Elizabeth on the World Wide Web to let her know a long, lost earl was coming to the palace. And locate a London tailor to outfit me properly to meet the royal family.

Naturally, as a descendent of the man who wrote all of the plays, I expect to be seated in the royal box for every performance of Shakespeare's plays at the Globe. As soon as I land in the British Isles, there's much work to do, starting with quitting the Liberal party and reregistering as a more splendid Conservative. Last but not least, when a Google search of the map of England locates my castle, I want it back!

GOOGLE GUIDE

Chapter 31: Who Was the Real Shakespeare?

For more on this subject, try these:

"The Shakespeare Conspiracy." (film). Time: 3:37 min.
Find title at YouTube: http://www.youtube.com/

"Genealogy and the Family Tree Researchers – The Google Toolbar."
(film). Time: 3:42 min. Find title at YouTube: http://www.youtube.
com/

"The Shakespeare Authorship Coalition." (web site). http://www.
doubtaboutwill.org/declaration/

For a longer listing, go to the book's web site:

Google Brain Book: http://googlebrainbook.blogspot.com/

Chapter 32

Are We There Yet?

Writing a book is an adventure.
To begin with, it is a toy and an amusement;
then it becomes a mistress; and then it becomes a master, and then a tyrant.
The last phase is that just as you are about to be reconciled to your servitude,
you kill the monster, and fling him to the public.

—Winston Churchill (1874-1965)

If you've seen *Groundhog Day*, the 1993 movie starring Bill Murray, you'll know why I can easily associate myself with Murray's predicament: He woke up one morning to find his life repeating itself day after day. What he had to deal with is exactly the problem a lot of us face: How to find a way to get out of a continuous time warp.

While most of us don't realize we're trapped by these repetitive events, since they take on a slightly different form each day, I guarantee you that keeping a careful record of your daily doings might help to reveal that a strange sameness is exactly what is happening to you, me, and a lot of people. Let me explain.

With each New Year arriving sooner than expected, as we get older, we become conscious of the passing of time. So naturally many of us are likely to consider making some new resolutions. We want to somehow take control of our lives and force ourselves to do better in the future. For me, it's to finish the *Great American Memoir*, which has been writing itself in my head for a long, long time.

For years I've been meaning to put it down on paper. And with another year always fast approaching, I am determined to set things right and resolve to get it done. So far it hasn't happened. But I keep telling myself that next year things ought to be different. Since the same thing seems to occur year after year—my book still needs to be finished—maybe the time has come to give this situation closer attention and re-examine the whole problem?

Why am I so frustrated? Because as time marches on, steadily day by day, I wake up each morning resolved to get started on the first chapter and then something happens that stops my doing what I'd intended. It's *Groundhog Day* all over again. After breakfast something very important needs to be done first. So I tell myself, "Take care of that and then you'll have time for the writing."

But no matter how hard I try, there's always something else. Yes, I could cite a long list of time-consuming demands, which certainly cannot be avoided. Example: doing my U.S. Income Tax. Admittedly that happens only once each year. But it's the kind of important task you simply can't avoid doing. It's not the only case. Add to the list the need to pay your property taxes, auto license renewal fees, or charge card bills, which seem to be constantly coming in.

You can't ignore these things. They're essentials. And as you grow older you find yourself making more frequent appointments to see the dentist, or doctor, going to the drug store to fill or refill medical prescriptions, or sending off letters to Congress to save Social Security or Medicare. So the day passes, and I again realize by nightfall that no work has been done on that anticipated masterpiece. By bedtime, I'm full of real anxiety.

Fearing that I'm apt not to sleep, I promise myself to do better the next day, drop off to sleep, and then find I'm still troubled by unfinished tasks in slumberland. My sleeping mind seems to burden me with work that seems oddly similar to my waking hours. The same type of theme keeps playing over and over. In my dreams I'm trying to repeatedly to get somewhere to complete some kind of project.

My nightmare forces me to keep moving—over mountains and down into valleys, up steams and down rivers, through alleys and down boulevards, never quite getting there. Undoubtedly Dr. Sigmund Freud would diagnose my subconscious as being preoccupied with "getting somewhere" or "getting something done."

The need to finish something—such as writing a book—has been going on longer than I care to admit. But believing a real writer needs to reveal "the inner man" to his reader, I must confess that my plan to write a book began at the age of twelve or thirteen, thanks to my early poetry and story-writing having been published in the Sunday supplement of the *Oakland Tribune* (which awarded books as prizes for poetry, stories, or drawings submitted by children).

The first typescript of that unfinished book may still be in an old trunk, but I don't have time to look for it. I'm too busy! But doing what, for heaven's sake? How did John Steinbeck and other creative artists like him ever get their writing done? Didn't they have leaky faucets, junk mail, unsolicited phone calls, and common ordinary things to chip away at their time? Somehow or another they must have said, "My writing comes first. To heck with having my car's oil changed every 5,000 miles."

My theory is that Mrs. John Steinbeck—or Mrs. Ernest Hemingway—did it all. When chores had to be done, their wives did it. That is, until they got sick and tired of the drudgery, the absence of their husbands, and walked out. Or if they were like Ariel Durant, who helped her husband Will Durant create the eleven-volume series, *The Story of Civilization*. For years she stuck it out and finally got credit as a co-author after helping him complete the sixth volume. But it didn't happen till the day Will Durant woke up to the fact his wife was a major contributor and told the publisher to make her a co-equal partner of all of his books.

Nobody knows how long the female sex has gone unsung for its share in men's accomplishments. It certainly must go back to the days when we lived in caves. Who knows what Mrs. Og did to help Mr. Og invent the wheel, discover fire, or plant that first marijuana seed (which gave us hemp to help make clothing)? Certainly she kept the children out of the way, allowing Mr. Og to say with satisfaction, "Ah, now I can concentrate on my great idea of rubbing two sticks together to see what happens."

Undoubtedly famous authors like Hemingway and Steinbeck received help from their wives, but it was costly—Ernest had four wives, which means three of them got tired of hearing him say, "Will you take care of that, honey?" or "Be a peach, dearest, and take the car into the garage for a lube job, so I can finish my book." As for John Steinbeck, he was married three times and recounts his wife-dependency in *Journal of a Novel,* the diary he kept while completing *East of Eden.*

While Norman Mailer holds the world's record for comings and goings of wives (having been married six times), what his marriage partners helped him accomplish is most impressive. According to last count the late eighty-one-year old author, pugilist, and iconoclast completed more than forty four works (books, film scripts, anthologies, etc.) before he'd gone through his first five wives, who obviously were fed up taking care of the chores.

Does this mean all writers must be married? Not necessarily so. But it helps to live in a hotel if the single life is for you. In a well-run hotel not much can happen to disturb your quiet tranquility, because you can always pick up the phone and tell the desk clerk, "Get someone up here pronto because the thermostat is on the blink and I'm getting cold." That's how George Santayana got his writing done. It was easy for this famous philosopher and novelist to write because he lived in hotels wherever he happened to be—London, Paris or Rome—and he ate all of his meals in the quiet of his room or at restaurants. Fortunately, he inherited enough money to permit this kind of lifestyle. But let's face it—you need a pile of money to pay someone else to do those needed chores. Believe me, it's more economical to find a willing helpmate to do it.

Knowing it's a careful balance between a happy marriage and a contented publisher, I've tried to strike a reasonable balance. While I've turned over a lot of necessary household duties to my wife in order to free myself for creative writing, I still find myself standing on a ladder to fix a broken smoke alarm, chopping wood to keep the stove going in winter, or tinkering with the toilet which won't stop running. It makes me feel like Alexander Graham Bell whenever I hear my wife call from the kitchen, "Come here, Gordon, I need you."

A real man would never ask a woman to do the really hard tasks, such as emptying wastepaper baskets or uncorking a bottle of wine. While I greatly admire William Shakespeare, he reputedly left his wife at home at Stratford upon Avon for months in order to scribble away at his plays in London. Or maybe he had a pint of grog at a nearby pub? The same can be said for Charles Dickens, who, despite his empathy for the weak and needy, never truly appreciated the contributions from his wife.

Writing a best seller isn't worth losing the one who keeps you going. Writers who accomplish anything need a companion by their side and, if they are smart, they will give them credit for the help they get. Thus I can add up all the data, analyze it, and come to only one conclusion––that to be forthright and honest, the byline atop this work should read: *By Gordon and Darlene Greb*. What I'm writing is no more my work alone than what ends up as the President's "State of the Union" address. Even the president needs somebody to do the five thousand mile checkup on the White House limousines, if he can ever hope to finish writing his speeches.

It's high time, in my own case, to give full credit to my darling wife for doing the chores that enable me to finish this book. I couldn't have written a word without her, my one and only chief cook and bottle washer. The problem at the moment is to find a plumber to fix that leaky faucet in the upstairs bathroom. If Darlene doesn't get someone soon to do it, how can I possibly finish a *Great American Memoir?*

GOOGLE GUIDE

Chapter 32: Are We There Yet?

For more on this subject, try these:

"I Could Write a Book – Frank Sinatra and Kim Novak." (song).
Find title at YouTube: http://www.youtube.com/

"Jeffrey Archer – Advice for Writers." (video). Time: 3:10
Find title at YouTube: http://www.youtube.com/

"Seven Million Words Later." Bruce Bliven talks to Gordon Greb.
(article). http://grebwithbliven.blogspot.com/

For a longer listing, go to the book's web site:

Google Brain Book: http://googlebrainbook.blogspot.com/

Acknowledgements

My google life has been exceedingly long because I've been blessed with good health in old age. I am indebted to a number of people for that, beginning with my ancestors' longevity genes and my guardian angel-like parents, who saw that I brushed my teeth and ate my carrots while growing up.

As an octogenarian, I could not have dreamed of completing this book without the loving care of my wife Darlene, who saw that I ate the right low-fat diet, got regular medical and dental checkups, and hit the pavement with shoe leather wherever we went, whether exploring the paths along Little Chico Creek, the high country of the Sierra Nevada, the streets of San Francisco, the myriad districts of London, or the mysteries of the Great Wall of China.

If I'd had any thoughts of spending my last days in a rocking chair, they were quickly dismissed by my former students, who realized the old professor wasn't as stuffy as an old maid but could be a funny old codger in his old age. I particularly want to thank Editor Ron Miller and his compatriots from San Jose State University who invited me to put my stuff alongside theirs on their Web site— www.thecolumnists. com —Elias Castillo, Joanne Engelhardt, Michael Johnson, Joyce Kiefer, and Gerald Nachman.

Thanks, too, to Jim Hummel, whose wonderful cartoons grace this book; Francine Miller, my overseas coordinator and ex officio London agent; Valerie Dickerson Morris, who took her campus news reporting to the anchor chair at CNN in New York; and also Bill Knowles, who rose from the position of an ABC network news executive to that of a distinguished university professor.

I also cannot forget editors who encouraged me like George Thompson of the *San Leandro News-Observer*, Jack Israel of the *Fort*

Dix Post, and Scott Newhall of the *San Francisco Chronicle*; professors like Berkeley's Robert W. Desmond, John Lund, and Phillip Griffin; Minnesota's Ralph Casey, Ralph Nafziger, Edward Emery, and Mitchell Charnley; and Stanford's Robert Walker, Phil Buck, Arnaud Levelle, Chick Bush, and Wilber Schramm.

If any of my innumerable writings and broadcasts still exist in recoverable form, I credit that fact to the technical skills of Glen Pensinger and Bob Reynolds of the SJSU's Instructional Television Center. Great assistance in preserving my work also was tendered by university colleagues Dick Lewis, Terry Martin, Dick Elliott, Jerry Kemp, Walt Fox, Ken Roed, Peter Buzanski, Clarence Flick, and Mike Adams.

I also thank the talent scout who hired me—chairman Dwight Bentel—and other journalism faculty members at San Jose State, who supported my grandiose plans for a radio-television news curriculum, Dennis Brown, Pierce Davies, Dolores Spurgeon, Dave Grey, and Joe Swan.

Remembered with fondness, too, are those graduates of mine who made their mark in the profession, returned to the university, and helped advance the goals by becoming journalism faculty in our school, notably Rik Whitaker, Darla Belshe, Ken Blase, Harvey Gotliffe, and Bill Briggs.

To my daughter Darla I'm grateful for editing this book with the same loving care she has devoted to the creative works of her own three children, and perhaps wondering, wouldn't her father's have been better if he'd used scissors, crayons, and a stapler?

In conclusion, it's my belief that if Google, Inc. finally achieves its goal, we will all be the richer for it. I hope future generations keep on googling and that through their use of all this new knowledge, we can make this world a better place to live in.

While it's been great fun trying to write the *Great American Memoir*, I must apologize to you now, dear reader, for any mistakes you'll find in my imperfect past, abjectly admit them, and promise next time to try to do better.

References

ONLINE BIBLIOGRAPHY

For additional links to each chapter's subject matter, go to the book's web site: http://googlebrainbook.blogspot.com/

Preface: **The Meaning of Google**

"The 'Google' Life." (CBS News).
http://www.cbsnews.com/video/watch/?id=4401791n&tag=content
Main;contentBody/

"Google's Master Plan." (film).
Find title at YouTube: http://www.youtube.com/related/

"History Detectives, Blue Print Special." (Gordon Greb on PBS).
http://www.pbs.org/opb/historydetectives/investigations/610_
blueprintspecial.html

Ch 1: **The Dog Ate What?**

"Meet the Obama Dog 03/30/209." (White House parody).
http://whitehouse.gov1.info/blog/blog_post/blog-obama-dog.html

"Tales of Yore: The Mail Carrier's Revenge", by Mark J. Woodbury.
(book). http://search.barnesandnoble.com/Tales-of-Yore/Mark-J-
Woodbury/

"Dreams from My Father: A Story of Race and Inheritance," by Barack Obama. (book). Find title at Google Books: http://books. google.com/

Ch 2: **Mind the Gap**

"On the Sunny Side of the Street," by Ted Lewis. (song). Find title at YouTube: http://www.youtube.com/

"'See America First,' Oakland, California – 1931." (film). http://www.archive.org/details/SeeAmeri1931/

"The U.S. Grant Connection: Sept. 1, 2008," by Gordon Greb. (column). http://www.thecolumnists.com/greb/greb51.html/

Ch 3: **Start Googling Now**

"King of Jazz: Part 1 of 3," by Bing Crosby with Rhythm Boys. (song). Time: 2:07 min. Find title at YouTube: http://www.youtube. com/

"Oakland, California -1928." (film). http://www.archive.org/details/OaklandC1928/

"Will Rogers on the Radio – Unemployment." (recording). Time: 2:45 min. Find title at YouTube: http://www.youtube.com/

Ch 4: **It's a Jungle Out There**

"Brother, Can You Spare a Dime," by Bing Crosby. (song). Find title at YouTube: http://www.youtube.com/

""National Recovery Administration – NRA Promo – 1933." (film). http://www.archive.org/details/National1933/

"Memoirs of a Sandlot Kid," by Gordon Greb. (column). http://www. thecolumnists.com/greb/greb16.html

Ch 5: **Goodbye, Old Man Depression**

"Happy Days Are Here Again," by Ben Selvin and the Crooners. (song). Find title at YouTube: http://www.youtube.com/

"FDR—The Man Who Changed America." (film). Find title at YouTube: http://www.youtube.com/

"Goodbye, Old Man Depression," by Gordon Greb. (column). http://www.thecolumnists.com/greb/greb23.html/

Ch 6: **Pick Yourself Up**

"Pick Yourself Up – Swing Time (1936)," by Fred Astaire and Ginger Rogers. (song). Time: 2:10 min. Find title at YouTube: http://www.youtube.com/

"Bullets or Ballots (1936)." (movie trailer). Find title at YouTube: http://www.youtube.com/

"The Brown Bomber vs. Hitler's Pride," by Stan Isaacs. (column). http://www.thecolumnists.com/isaacs/isaacs3B05.html/

Ch 7: **Who's Afraid of the Big Bad Wolf?**

"Who's Afraid of the Big, Bad Wolf?" (song). Find title at YouTube: http://www.youtube.com/

Newsreel: "All-American Soap Box Derby (1936)." (newsreel). Find title at YouTube: http://www.youtube.com/

"San Francisco General Strike Newsreel 1/2 (1934)." (newsreel). Find title at YouTube: http://www.youtube.com/

Ch 8: **Bugs 'n' Things**

"My First Summer in the Sierra," by John Muir. (book).

Find title at Google Books: http://books.google.com/

"Roosevelt Addresses Boy Scouts (1935)." (newsreel).
http://www.archive.org/details/1935-02-11_Roosevelt_Addresses_
Boy_Scouts/

"Bugs 'n' Things," by Gordon Greb. (column).
http://bugthings.blogspot.com/

Ch 9: A Gentleman of the Press

"The Front Page - Original Trailer 1974." (movie trailer).
Find title at YouTube: http://www.youtube/

"Newspaper Story (1950)." (encyclopedia film). Time: 16:29 min.
http://www.archive.org/details/NewspaperSto/

"The Golden Gate International Exposition (1939)." (home movie).
http://www.archive.org/details/Californ1939/

Ch 10: The America I saw in 1941

"'Duke Ellington: 'Take the "A" Train.'" (song).
Find title at YouTube: http://www.youtube.com/

"His Girl Friday (1940)" (Columbia feature length film) Time: 92
min. http://www.archive.org/details/his girl_friday/

"Robert Benchley and the Knights of the Algonquin." (film).
Find title at YouTube: http://www.youtube.com/watch?v=64-
15TwZnJU/

Ch 11: Prisoner in a Chinese Cookie Factory

"WWII – Day of Infamy – Japan Bombs Pearl Harbor." (film). Time:
7:57 min. Find title at YouTube: http://www.youtube.com/

"Edward R, Murrow from London – 1942." (CBS audio).
http://www.archive.org/details/murrow_in_london_1942/

"Troop Train (1943)." (U.S. government film)
http://www.archive.org/details/TroopTra1943/

Ch 12: **A Movie They Didn't Want Us to See**

"Scarlet Street (1945)." (Universal feature length film). Time: 102
min.http://www.archive.org/details/ScarletStreet/

"History Detectives, Blue Print Special." (Gordon Greb on
PBS program). http://www.pbs.org/opb/historydetectives/
investigations/610_blueprintspecial.html

"Bonhoeffer: Jamming the wheels of the Nazi war machine." (film).
10:03 min. Find title at YouTube: http://www.youtube.com/

Ch 13: **Homecoming**

"21 Nazi Chiefs Guilty, Nuremberg Trials 1946/10/8." (newsreel).
Time: 4:46 min. Find title at YouTube: http://www.youtube.com/

"The USO Honors the Military as told by Bob Hope." (film).
Find title at YouTube: http://www.youtube.com/

"The Further Adventures of Rusty, Boy Aviator: April 4, 2005,"
by Gordon Greb. (column). http://www.thecolumnists.com/greb/
greb14.html/

Ch 14: **Where Do We Go From Here?**

"Broadway 1950s New York City at Night." (film).
Find title at YouTube: http://www.youtube.com/

"Teletours San Francisco 1950 Man on the Street." (film).
Find title at YouTube: http://www.youtube.com/

"The Greb Report: Special Anniversary Edition." (web site). http://www.grebreport.blogspot.com/

Ch 15: **My Own Fight With McCarthyism**

"The Tennessee Waltz – Singer Patti Page 1950." (song).
Find title at YouTube: http://www.youtube.com/

"Edward R. Murrow." (film). Time: 6:21 min.
Find title at YouTube: http://www.youtube.com/

"Undefeated and Uninvited." (film).
Find title at YouTube: http://www.youtube.com/

Ch 16: **Hollywood Finds a Miracle**

"The Professor's Reel Life," by Gordon Greb. (column).
http://www.thecolumnists.com/greb/greb65.html/

"Robert Benchley: Home Movies." (film).
Find title at YouTube: http://www.youtube.com//

"Children and the Movies: Media Influences and the Payne Fund Controversy," by Garth S. Jowett, Ian C. Jarvie, and Kathryn H. Fuller. (book).
Find title at Google Books: http://books.google.com/

Ch 17: **I Help Democrats Win**

"Reagan Campaigns for Truman in 1948." (film). Time: 4:14 min.
Find title at YouTube: http://www.youtube.com/

"Will Rogers on Congress." (film). Time: 2:35 min.
Find title at YouTube: http://www.youtube.com/

"Is There a Better Way to Choose Our Leader?" by Gordon Greb. (column). http://www.thecolumnists.com/greb/greb8.html/

Ch 18: **Your Big Scoop Can Hurt Us**

"Citizen Kane – How to Run a Newspaper." (film). Time: 2:29 min. http://www.youtube.com/watch?v=tzhb3U2cONs/

"We Take You Now to the United Nations," by Gordon Greb. (script). http://grebscoop.blogspot.com/

"Do's and Don'ts for Beginning Writers," by Gordon Greb. (magazine article). http://grebsyndicate.blogspot.com/

Ch 19: **Eureka! I Find the First Broadcaster**

"The Platters 'Remember When' 1959." (song).
Find title at YouTube: http://www.youtube.com/

"The First Lady of Broadcasting," interview by Gordon Greb. (text). http://grebdiscovery.blogspot.com/

"Charles Herrold, Inventor of Radio Broadcasting," by Gordon Greb and Mike Adams. (book). Find title at Google Books: http://books.google.com/

Ch 20: **War and Peace on Campus**

"The Beatles – Here Comes the Sun." (song).
Find title at YouTube: http://www.youtube.com/

"Ronald Reagan Versus The Hippies." (television). Time: 2:00 min. Find title at YouTube: http://www.youtube.com/

"You and Public Relations," by Gordon Greb. (text). http://grebtv.blogspot.com/

Ch 21: **Imbecile in France**

"How to Speak French." (film). Time: 3:52 min.
Find title at YouTube: http://www.youtube.com/

"Metropole Paris email from Gordon Greb: Paris: It's for Old Lovers, Too." http://www.metropoleparis.com/1998/304/email304.html/

"Dover Ferry Crossing to Calais, France." (film). Time: 2:11 min. Find title at YouTube: http://www.youtube.com/

Ch 22: **Lost in China: Help, Marco Polo**

"Learn Chinese – Speak Chinese – My name is and I am from." (film). Time: 2:12 min. Find title at YouTube: http://www.youtube.com/

"President Nixon goes to China – Part 17 of 28." (film). Find title at YouTube: http://www.youtube.com/

"Learn Chinese with NBC's Show Al Roker at WLE China Study abroad Beijing campus." (film). Time: 5:48 min. Find title at YouTube: http://www.youtube.com/

Ch 23: **A Philosopher Learns to Laugh**

"Monty Python – Meaning of Life (Fighting Each Other)." (film). Find title at YouTube: http://www.youtube.com/

"A Writer's Philosophy of Life," by Gordon Greb. (text). http://grebphilosophy.blogspot.com/

"Robert Benchley...That Inferior Feeling."(film). Time: 9:08 min. Find title at YouTube: http://www.youtube.com/

Ch 24: **I'm a Yankee Doodle Dandy**
"Yankee Doodle Dandy 1942 Trailer." (movie trailer) Find title at YouTube: http://www.youtube.com/

"Cold War Revisited - 1961 Interview," by Gordon Greb. (kinescope). Find title at YouTube: http://www.youtube.com/

"JibJab.com – This Land." (animated cartoon).
http://www.youtube.com/watch?v=z8Q-sRdV7SY&feature=related/

Ch 25: **How I Quit Smoking**

"Tex Williams Smoke Smoke Smoke (That Cigarette)." (song).
Find title at YouTube: http://www.youtube.com/

"The Golden Age of Cigarette Advertising." (film).
Find title at YouTube: http://www.youtube.com/

"Billy Sunday Preaching About Alcohol." (sermon). Time: 2:22 min.
Find title on YouTube: http://www.youtube.com/

Ch 26: **Welcome to the Twenty-First Century**

"New Years Eve 2000-2001 ABC – WBZ." (television).
Find title at YouTube: http://www.youtube.com/

"Looking Backward: 2000 – 1887," by Edward Bellamy. (book).
Find title at Google Books: http://books.google.com/

"Season's Greetings from a Golden Oldie," by Gordon Greb.
(column). http://www.thecolumnists.com/greb/greb57.html

Ch 27: **The Man Who Would Be King**

"George Bush on Social Security." (CNBC)
Find title at YouTube: http://www.youtube.com/

"The Man Who Would be King," by Stuart Taylor Jr. (article).
Atlantic Monthly, April 2006)http://www.theatlantic.com/
doc/200604/bush-autocracy/

"Halloween on Wall Street: Oct. 27, 2008, by Gordon Greb.
(column). http://www.thecolumnists.com/greb/greb54.html/
Ch 28: **Is Orwell's 1984 Already Here?**

"1984 By George Orwell, 1949." (Planet eBook).
http://www.planetebook.com/1984.asp/

"Newspeak from the Recent Attacks 2001-09-13." (Newspeak
dictionary). http://www.newspeakdictionary.com/ns_frames.html/

"It's the 'New' Old World': March 14, 2005," by Gordon Greb.
(column). http://www.thecolumnists.com/greb/greb12.html/

Ch 29: Lord, Give Me My Daily Paper

"Bill Moyers: What's Wrong with Big Media." (video).
Find title at YouTube:http://www.youtube.com/

"Fame, My Son, is Not for Editors," by Gordon Greb. (article).
http://grebandson.blogspot.com/

"JibJab – What We Call the News." (animated cartoon).
Find title at YouTube: http://www.youtube.com/

Ch 30: Walter Mitty, Cary Grant, and Me

"The Secret Life of Walter Mitty [1]." (film). Time: 9:53 min.
Find title at YouTube: fhttp://www.youtube.com/

"Cary Grant: A Class Apart," by Graham McCann. (book).
See quotation on page xi: "Everybody wants to be Cary Grant..."
Find title at Google Books: http://books.google.com/

"Silents, Please!: Feb. 21, 2005," by Gordon Greb. (column).
http://www.thecolumnists.com/greb/greb10.html/

Ch 31: Who Was the Real Shakespeare?

"The Shakespeare Conspiracy." (film) Time: 3:37 min.
Find title at YouTube: http://www.youtube.com/

"Genealogy and the Family Tree Researchers – The Google Toolbar." (film) Time: 3:42 min. Find title at YouTube: http://www.youtube. com/

"The Shakespeare Authorship Coalition." (web site). http://www.doubtaboutwill.org/declaration/

Ch 32: **Are We There Yet?**

"I Could Write a Book – Frank Sinatra and Kim Novak." (song). Find title at YouTube: http://www.youtube.com/

"Jeffrey Archer – Advice for Writers." (video). Time: 3:10 min. Find title at YouTube: http://www.youtube.com/

"Seven Million Words Later." Bruce Bliven talks to Gordon Greb. (article). http://grebwithbliven.blogspot.com/

IN PRINT BIBLIOGRAPHY

BOOKS

Anderson, Mark. *Shakespeare by Another Name.* New York: Gotham Books, 2006.

Bagdikian, Ben H. *Double Vision.* Boston: Beacon Press, 1995.

Baker, Russell. *Growing Up.* New York: New American Library, 1982.

Bettmann, Otto L. *The Delights of Reading: Quotes, Notes, & Anecdotes.* Boston: David R. Godine, Publisher, Inc., 1987.

Bernard, Andre. *Now All We Need Is a Title: Famous Book Titles and How They Got That Way.* New York: W. W. Norton & Company, 1995.

Bernstein, Matthew. *Controlling Hollywood: Censorship and Regulation in the Studio Era.* New Brunswick: Rutgers University Press, 1999.

Blackbeard, Bill, Dale Crain, and James Vance. *100 Years of Comic Strips*. New York: Barnes & Noble Books, 1995.

Bok, Edward Bok. *The Americanization of Edward Bok*. New York: Pocket Books, Inc., 1965.

Carpenter, Patricia F. and Paul Totah, eds. *San Francisco Fair: Treasure Island 1939-40*. San Francisco: Scottwall Associates, 1989.

Crane, Clarkson. *The Western Shore*. Salt Lake City: Gibbs M. Smith, Inc., 1985.

Cooke, Alistair. *Alistair Cooke's American Journey: Life on the Home Front in the Second World War*. London: Penguin Books, 2006.

Dille, Robert C. Dille, ed. *The Collected Works of Buck Rogers in the 25th Century*. New York: Chelsea House, 1980.

Evanosky, Dennis and Eric J. Kos. *East Bay: Then and Now*. San Diego: Thunder Bay Press, 2004.

Friedman, Rosemary. *A Writer's Commonplace Book*. London: Michael O'Mara Books Limited, 2006.

Frank, Leonard Roy. *Random House Webster's Wit & Humor Quotationary*. New York: Random House, 2000.

Flamm, Jerry. *Good Life in Hard Times: San Francisco's '20s and '30s*. San Francisco: Chronicle Books, 1977.

Gabler, Neal. *Walt Disney: The Triumph of the American Imagination*. New York: Vintage Books, 2007.

Greene, Bob. *Once Upon a Town*. New York: HarperCollins, 2003.

Greb, Gordon. *The Benbow Family, California Pioneers*. Chico: Sky Mountain Circle, 1994.

_____. *Freedom of the Movies in Presenting News and Opinions*, master's thesis (unpublished). Minneapolis: University of Minnesota, 1951.

_____and Mike Adams. *Charles Herrold: Inventor of Radio Broadcasting*. Jefferson, NC; McFarland Publishers, 2003.

Halberstam, David. *The Fifties*. New York: Ballantine Books, 1994.

Hynes, Samuel. *The Growing Seasons: An American Boyhood Before the War*. New York: Viking, 2003.

Lehrer, Jonah. *Proust Was a Neuroscientist*. New York: Houghton Mifflin Co., 2007.

Lillibridge, G.D. *The Innocent Years: Growing Up in a Small Town in the 1920s and 1930s*. Huron: East Eagle Company, 1994.

Kennedy, David. *Freedom from Fear: The American People in Depression and War, 1929-1945*. New York: Oxford University Press, 2001.

MacDonald, Fred J. *Don't Touch That Dial: Radio Programming in American Life from 1920 to 1960*. Chicago: Nelson-Hall, 1991.

Manchester, William Manchester. *The Glory and the Dream: A Narrative History of America, 1932-1972*. New York: Bantam Books, 1979.

Mill, John Stuart. *On Liberty*. David Spitz (ed.). New York: W.W. Norton and Co., 1975.

Miller, Webb. *I Found No Peace*. New York: Simon and Schuster, 1936.

Neill, George W. *Infantry Soldier: Holding the Line at the Battle of the Bulge*. Norman: University of Oklahoma Press, 2000.

Obama, Barack. *Dreams from My Father*. New York: Three Rivers Press, 2004.

Pyle, Ernie. *Home Country*. New York: William Sloane Associates, Inc., 1947.

Rauchway, Eric. *The Great Depression and the New Deal: A Very Short Introduction*. New York: Oxford University Press, 2008.

Reinhardt, Richard. *Treasure Island: San Francisco's Exposition Years*. San Francisco: Scrimshaw Press, 1973.

Robinson, James. *The Mind in the Making*. New York: Harper & Brothers Publishers, 1939.

Robinson, Jerry. *The Comics: An Illustrated History of Comic Strip Art*. New York: G.P. Putnam's Sons, 1974.

Shirer, William L. *Berlin Diary: The Journal of a Foreign Correspondent, 1934-1941*. Tess Press, 1941.

Shute, Henry A. *The Real Diary of a Real Boy*. Whitefish, MT: Kessinger Publishing, 2005.

Smith, Elsdon C. *New Dictionary of American Family Names*. New York: Grammercy Publishing Co., 1988.

Sperling, John. *Rebel with a Cause*. New York: John Wiley & Sons, Inc., 2000.

Stross, Randall. *Planet Google*. New York: Free Press, 2008.

Thomas, William E., ed. *Front Page: A Collection of Historical Headlines from the Los Angeles Times, 1881-1987*. New York: Harry N. Abrams, Inc., 1987.

Turkel, Studs. *Hard Times: An Oral History*. New York: Pantheon, 1970.

Wolf, Naomi. *The End of America: Letter of Warning to a Young Patriot.* White River Junction, VT: Chelsea Green Publishing, 2007.

ARTICLES, JOURNALS, AND CORRESPONDENCE

Greb, Gordon. "Bugs 'n' Things." *Scout Scribe.* Oakland: Boy Scouts of America, May 1938.

—————. "My 1941 Trip." Diary of a railroad journey around the United States, 1941. (Private collection, unpublished).

Correspondence with Ephraim S. London, counselor at law, London, Simpson, and London, 150 Broadway, New York, N.Y., 1952

NEWSPAPERS

Los Angeles Times
Oakland Tribune
Oakland Post Enquirer
San Francisco Chronicle
San Jose Mercury News
Sacramento Bee